# KRISTEN PARKER

# Between the Ember and the Tide

First edition

This book was professionally typeset on Reedsy.
Find out more at reedsy.com

# Contents

**One**

# The Prophecy Awakens

The wind in Emberfall was always fierce—wild, untamed, like the fire coursing through Caelan's veins. It roared through the craggy peaks that separated his kingdom from the distant waters of Tidewell, carrying with it the scents of burning embers, ash, and the ever-present reminder that the fire was both his gift and his curse.

Caelan stood atop the high cliffs of Emberfall's capital, overlooking the molten river that snaked through the valley below. His cloak whipped in the wind, the crimson fabric billowing like a living thing, an extension of the flames that seethed beneath his skin. He could feel them—the fire, always present, always hungry. The very air seemed to vibrate with its restless energy.

It had been a long time since Caelan had felt the need to prove his strength to anyone. His reputation as one of the most skilled fire mages in Emberfall was well established.

But something had changed in the past few days. An ancient tension had begun to coil in his gut, something more than the fire that raged within him.

It had all started with the ancient text, the one buried deep in the royal archives. Caelan had found it by chance—an accidental slip of parchment as he searched for a record of an old battle strategy. The words, written in a language older than time, had jumped off the page in a way Caelan couldn't explain. He'd been drawn to them, unable to resist. And then he'd found the prophecy.

*Two souls shall rise, the flame and the tide. United, they must stand, or the world shall burn.*

The words had burned themselves into his memory, etched like a brand on his mind. But what chilled him to his core was the second part of the prophecy, the part he couldn't ignore: *The one who wields the flame shall find the water, and the water will guide the flame. Their union shall either save or destroy all that is.*

It made no sense. Fire and water—two opposing forces. In the history of Emberfall, no mage had ever been able to harness both. The two elements were sworn enemies, a constant struggle for dominance, as natural as day and night. The prophecy was madness.

But still, something in Caelan's chest had tightened. He could not ignore it.

The wind howled around him as he made his way down the stone steps leading from the castle. The castle had been built into the very cliffs, its towers rising like obsidian spires from the rock. The walls were covered in deep fissures, remnants of long-forgotten battles with the Tidewell mages. The bitter rivalry between fire and water ran deeper than the rivers themselves.

As he walked, Caelan's thoughts remained with the prophecy. He had to admit, it unsettled him. He had never believed in fate or destiny. Magic was a force of will—something to be mastered and controlled. And yet, the words haunted him. They had led him to seek out the greatest scholars of his kingdom, the mages who had studied the ancient arts.

"What does it mean?" Caelan had asked, his voice sharp, as he held the parchment before them.

One by one, they had looked at the prophecy with confusion, each unwilling to speak the words aloud. Finally, it was the head mage, Master Tyrus, who had broken the silence. His eyes had been heavy with dread.

"Fire and water," Tyrus had muttered. "An impossible union. A myth, one spoken of only in whispers."

"But it's real," Caelan had insisted. "I've seen it."

The old mage's eyes had narrowed, his hands shaking as he gripped the ancient scroll. "You must seek her out, Caelan. If the prophecy is true, she is the key."

And now, standing on the cliffs overlooking the valley, Caelan knew that he had no choice but to follow the call of the prophecy. Somewhere, out there, across the treacherous lands that separated Emberfall from Tidewell, was the woman the prophecy spoke of. Lyra.

He didn't believe in fate. But fate, it seemed, believed in him.

The storm had come quickly.

It wasn't unusual for Emberfall to be struck by sudden storms, the winds shifting unpredictably, sometimes turning violent in an instant. But this—this felt different. The sky had darkened ominously, the clouds swirling in unnatural patterns, thick and heavy. A distant rumble of thunder echoed, the low growl reverberating through the earth, as though the very ground trembled in anticipation.

Caelan had always been able to sense when something wasn't right. And this, this was wrong.

The air was thick with the scent of ozone, and the distant crash of thunder was followed by a flicker of light on the horizon—bright, electric, blinding. It was the kind of storm that spoke of ancient power, forces beyond mortal control. His instincts told him that this was no ordinary storm.

And then, through the chaos of the wind and rain, he saw her.

She stood at the edge of the cliffs, her figure barely visible through the mist, a silhouette outlined by the flashes of lightning. The wind tossed her dark hair about her face, and her presence seemed to pulse with a quiet power. The water mage. Lyra.

Caelan's breath caught in his throat.

She was everything he had imagined, and yet nothing at all. There was an ethereal quality to her that made her seem as if she belonged to the storm itself—like she was both of it and apart from it, a part of nature's fury.

She turned, and their gazes locked. Her eyes—striking, intense, a storm of their own—met his with a mixture of curiosity and wariness. There was a flicker of recognition between them, something that neither of them could deny. The prophecy had been right. They were bound together.

The storm raged louder as if in response to their meeting, the winds howling and the lightning crashing closer, as if nature itself was eager for their union—or perhaps eager to tear them apart. Caelan's pulse quickened, his fire instinctively rising, the flames licking at his skin, just beneath the surface.

"What is this?" Lyra's voice rang out, her words barely audible over the howling wind. She was barely twenty feet away from him, and yet it felt as though an ocean separated them.

"I don't know," Caelan replied, his voice thick with tension. "But it's real, isn't it? The prophecy. You're the one."

Lyra took a step closer, her presence both calming and dangerous. "I'm not the one you think I am," she said, her voice colder now, carrying a trace of something deeper, something unknown. "And I'm not here because of some prophecy. I'm here because of you."

Her words sent a shiver down his spine. He could see it now—the flickers of water that seemed to dance around her, invisible but undeniably present. She controlled the tide, and Caelan could feel its power thrumming in the air.

"What do you want from me?" Lyra's gaze never left him, the storm swirling around her, as though she was at the heart of it all.

Caelan's fingers twitched, the fire rising within him in response to her power. He fought to contain it, to not let the flames take control. "I don't know," he admitted, his voice low and tense. "But I think we need each other. The prophecy—"

"The prophecy is a lie," she interrupted, her voice suddenly sharp. "A cruel trick meant to manipulate you, Caelan. We are enemies, nothing more."

The words stung, but Caelan refused to let them wound him. He had known, deep down, that it wasn't going to be easy. The fire and the water, the flame and the tide—they were opposites, bound by a fate neither of them had asked for. But there was something in her eyes that made him hesitate, something that spoke of a deeper truth.

"Then why are you here?" he asked, the question lingering in the heavy air between them.

Lyra hesitated, her eyes flickering with something unreadable. "I'm here because I can feel it too, Caelan. The prophecy… It's not just your destiny, it's mine. We're bound together, whether we like it or not."

The words struck him like a blow. He had known it, sensed it, but hearing her admit it—he hadn't expected that.

A crack of thunder split the air, and the ground beneath them trembled. The storm was upon them now, wild and untamable. Caelan could feel the storm in his bones, the energy in the air responding to their confrontation. It was as if the world itself was waiting for them to make a decision.

And then Lyra spoke again, her voice barely audible over the wind. "We don't have much time. You need to come with me, Caelan. The storm is only the beginning."

He looked into her eyes, his heart racing, his body alive with fire. The storm raged on around them, but in this moment, the world seemed to stop. This was the start of something neither of them could control, something that would either save them—or destroy them.

Caelan took a deep breath, his fire crackling beneath his skin, and stepped forward.

"Then let's see it through," he said, his voice firm. "Together."

And with that, the storm closed in around them, the fire and water meeting at the edge of the world, where destiny awaited.

The storm roared around them, a cacophony of wind and lightning that seemed to press in on Caelan from all sides. He could feel the pulse of his magic—the fire, always so eager to break free, surging beneath his skin. It tugged at him, like a restless animal, but the storm was something else entirely. It was as if the air itself was charged with a power far greater than either fire or water, something primordial. Something ancient.

Lyra's eyes were locked on his, and in them Caelan saw a reflection of his own turmoil. Her magic, the water, was just as restless. It lapped at the edges of his fire like a tide, cautious yet constant, as though testing the limits of what they could share. He could feel the weight of her gaze, and it made his heart race faster, his pulse thudding in his ears. She was beautiful, but it was more than that—there was something inside of her, something deeper than her control over the water, something that called to him.

But there was a distance between them, something invisible that both kept them apart and drew them together. Caelan knew it, and he could see it in her eyes too.

"Where do we go from here?" His voice cut through the storm, low and uncertain, despite the surge of fire that filled him. "What are we supposed to do?"

Lyra didn't immediately answer. She stepped closer, her movements graceful despite the storm raging around them, her feet barely making a sound on the rocky ground. The water that she controlled swirled gently around her feet like an unseen current, the wetness of the earth reflecting her presence.

"I don't know," she finally whispered, almost to herself. "But I do know one thing—we can't ignore this. The storm… it's only the beginning."

The wind howled louder, carrying with it an eerie resonance. The distant horizon flickered with flashes of lightning, the night sky torn apart by sudden, violent bursts of light. Caelan felt the weight of it—this was no ordinary storm. This was the storm that had been foretold, the one that marked the beginning of everything they both feared.

"You said the prophecy was a lie," Caelan said, the words heavy on his tongue. "But then you came here. You knew it was true, didn't you?"

Lyra didn't look away. Her gaze held his for a long moment, and then she nodded. Her eyes were stormy, shifting with something Caelan couldn't fully understand—something raw and fragile.

"I thought it was a lie," she said quietly, her voice barely audible over the wind. "But then… I felt it. In the water. In the storm. It calls to me, Caelan. Just as it calls to you."

Caelan felt his chest tighten. Her words were a mirror of his own feelings, though they didn't make the situation any easier to bear. He didn't want this. He didn't want to be tied to her, to this prophecy, to the war that loomed between fire and water. And yet, the more he tried to deny it, the more undeniable the connection between them became.

He took a step closer, his boots crunching against the gravel as the wind threatened to whip him off balance. He could feel the heat of his magic rising, the flames licking at his skin, a dangerous, crackling energy. He fought to control it, but it wasn't easy when she was so near, when she seemed to pull the fire from him as naturally as she drew the water from the depths of the earth.

"What happens if we can't control it?" Caelan asked, his voice rough. He had to know. This wasn't just about them anymore. It was about everything—about the prophecy, about the world they had both inherited and now seemed doomed to change.

"Then everything ends," Lyra replied softly, her expression unreadable. She stepped even closer to him now, so close that the edges of her cloak brushed against his. The coldness of the water that followed her was a sharp contrast to the heat that enveloped him. "This is bigger than us, Caelan. The water and the fire—they are both ancient, and they're both powerful. But if they're not united… if they don't find balance…"

"Then the world will burn," Caelan finished for her, his voice dark with the weight of those words.

Her eyes flickered with something like fear, but it was gone as quickly as it came. "Yes."

The wind picked up again, gusting fiercely, as though urging them both forward. Lyra took another step toward him, her breath coming faster now. "We need to go to the heart of the storm. We can't stay here."

Before Caelan could respond, the ground beneath them shook violently, a rumble so deep it felt like the earth itself was coming undone. The storm intensified, the winds howling with even more fury. Caelan could feel the air around him rippling, the very atmosphere alive with magic. The fire inside him surged again, but this time, it didn't feel like it was entirely his own. He glanced at Lyra, and for the first time, he saw it clearly—the water magic, flowing through her, coursing like liquid silver in the air between them.

Her power was a mirror to his. And it was wild.

"Now!" Lyra shouted, her voice lost in the roar of the storm.

Without thinking, Caelan grabbed her hand, the heat from his touch searing into her skin, but she didn't recoil. Instead, she held on tightly, her fingers cold against his burning skin. Together, they moved, their steps fast and sure as the storm around them raged.

They ran, the wind battering their faces, the light from the storm flashing so close it was as though the heavens themselves were splitting apart. The earth trembled beneath their feet, but they pushed forward.

They ran until there was no more ground left to stand on, until the cliffs disappeared beneath them, until they were standing at the edge of the world.

Caelan's heart pounded in his chest. The heat of his magic was overwhelming, but something inside of him, some instinct, kept him grounded. He could feel the pull of Lyra's power, the way the water swirled beneath her feet, pulling and pushing against his own fire. It was like being caught between two opposing forces, and yet, in that moment, he didn't care. All he knew was that he had to keep moving, that the storm had brought them here for a reason.

They stood at the precipice of something vast, something neither of them fully understood. Below them, the world stretched out like an uncharted ocean. And ahead—shrouded in the swirling storm—was the path that would either bind them forever or tear them apart.

"I don't know how we'll survive this," Caelan said, his voice a hoarse whisper as the wind whipped around them.

Lyra turned to face him, her expression softening for the first time. She looked at him as if seeing him for the first time, not as a fire mage or a stranger, but as someone she was bound to, someone she might just have to trust.

"We'll survive together," she said. "But we'll need each other. More than you realize."

The words lingered between them as the storm seemed to pause, the air stilling for a heartbeat before the next flash of lightning split the sky.

And then they moved together, into the unknown.
Into the heart of the storm.

# Two

# The Tide's Secret

The night was still, save for the steady crashing of waves against the jagged rocks below the cliff. Lyra stood at the edge of the precipice, her dark hair whipping around her face, her figure outlined by the faint silver light of the crescent moon. The ocean stretched endlessly before her, a dark, endless expanse of water, both beautiful and terrifying in its vastness.

Her heart beat in time with the rhythm of the waves, each crash against the rocks below reverberating deep within her bones. It was the same rhythm that had always calmed her, soothed her when she was overwhelmed, when she needed to escape the chaos of the world. But tonight, it did little to ease the storm inside her.

The prophecy. The fire mage. Caelan.

She had never imagined her life would become entwined with someone like him, someone from the enemy kingdom of

Emberfall. But here they were, standing at the edge of destiny, and neither of them was sure whether it was a destiny they could survive.

Lyra closed her eyes and let the wind tug at her cloak, its salty scent mingling with the faint, burning undertones of Caelan's fire. She could feel the heat of him even now, just a few paces away. He had a way of filling the air around him, making her pulse quicken, and her heart—foolishly—felt lighter than it had in months.

"You seem lost in thought," Caelan's voice broke through the quiet night, rough and filled with unspoken tension.

Lyra turned to face him, her pulse picking up again as she looked into his storm-gray eyes. There was something in them, something that seemed to see straight through her, peeling away her carefully constructed walls. She took a steadying breath, forcing her emotions back into check.

"I was thinking about how quickly my life has changed," she said softly, not quite meeting his gaze. "How everything seems to be falling apart."

"Falling apart?" Caelan's brow furrowed. He stepped closer, his presence a burning force she could feel even from a distance. "What are you talking about, Lyra?"

Lyra shook her head, her lips curling into a bitter smile. "You wouldn't understand."

"Try me." His tone was insistent, and there was something in the way he said it, a quiet plea for her to share her burden.

She hesitated, the weight of her secret pressing down on her chest. There were things she had kept hidden from him, things she wasn't ready to share. But the bond between them was undeniable. The fire and the water—they had been drawn together by forces beyond their control. And maybe, just maybe, Caelan deserved to know.

"I was born in Tidewell," she began, her voice tight. "My family, we were once powerful. My mother was one of the most respected mages in the kingdom. But then…" She trailed off, her thoughts drifting back to the day it all changed—the day the monarchy had turned on her, recognizing her growing power as a threat.

"Then what?" Caelan urged, taking another step toward her.

Lyra exhaled slowly, her gaze fixed on the horizon. "Then they began to fear us. My family was hunted. My mother… she was taken by the council." Her voice faltered, and she clenched her fists. "I was just a child, but I could still feel it— her power, her magic, draining from her. The water was what they wanted, Caelan. It's what they'll always want."

The waves crashed against the rocks below with a violent hiss, as though nature itself was reacting to her words. Caelan's gaze softened, and he reached out, placing a hand on her shoulder. The warmth of his touch was a stark contrast to the cold, briny air that clung to her skin.

"You're afraid they'll come for you again," he said, his voice low, almost a whisper.

She nodded, swallowing hard. "Yes. But that's not even the worst part. My power—it's growing, Caelan. Faster than I can control it." She turned toward him now, her eyes filled with fear. "I can't stop it. And I fear that, if I can't find a way to control it soon, I might destroy everything I touch. I might destroy you."

The words hung between them like a curse. Lyra took a step back, as though afraid of the very magic she was bound to.

"You said your power is… growing uncontrollably," Caelan said carefully. "What do you mean?"

She glanced down at her hands, the water around her feet swaying gently in response to her every movement. She could feel it, the magic inside her, restless and chaotic, like a storm waiting to break free. "It's like… like a tide that's too strong to hold back," she murmured. "The water is rising, and I can feel it wanting to burst forth. It's as if something inside me is calling to it—something ancient, something tied to the prophecy."

Caelan's face hardened. "The prophecy," he repeated, his voice tinged with disbelief. "You think it's because of the prophecy?"

"I don't know," Lyra admitted, her eyes darkening with uncertainty. "But I think… it's all connected. I think the prophecy has been leading us toward this moment." She paused, and when she spoke again, her voice was barely a whisper. "And I think we're running out of time."

Her words hit Caelan like a blow. The storm in his chest roared louder, his fire flaring up inside him. He could feel the tension rising between them, the connection that was both a blessing and a curse.

"I don't know what to do with this," Lyra continued, her voice shaking. "And I don't know if I can control it much longer."

Before Caelan could respond, the sound of rustling came from behind them—soft but unmistakable.

Lyra's heart leapt in her chest, and she spun around just in time to see the shadowy figures emerging from the darkness, their eyes glinting in the moonlight. Their movements were swift and calculated, like wolves closing in on their prey.

Assassins.

A cold surge of panic rushed through her veins. She had known this moment was coming, had known they wouldn't be safe for long. But the fear still struck her, sharp and unforgiving.

"Caelan," she hissed, grabbing his arm. "We have to run. Now."

He barely had time to respond before they were surrounded. The assassins emerged from the shadows, their forms clad in dark robes that fluttered around them like a second skin. They moved with deadly grace, their hands already reaching for their weapons—daggers, poisoned blades, things Lyra had learned to fear in her years of exile.

One of the assassins, a tall man with cruel, narrow eyes, stepped forward, a sneer twisting his lips. "You've been a thorn in the side of Tidewell for far too long, Lyra," he said, his voice smooth, cold. "It's time for you to come with us."

Lyra's heart raced. She didn't want to fight. She couldn't afford to lose control—not now, not with Caelan so close. But she wasn't about to let them take her without a fight.

"I won't go with you," she said, her voice low, dangerous.

The assassin chuckled darkly. "You don't have a choice." He snapped his fingers, and the others closed in, their movements synchronized as they raised their weapons.

Caelan's hand shot out, and before Lyra could react, he was already engulfed in flames. The heat of it was intense, a bright, searing burst of light that pushed the assassins back, forcing them to stumble.

But they didn't retreat.

Lyra could feel the water stirring within her, pushing at the edges of her control. She needed to act fast. Her hand shot out, her magic surging with a powerful force, and a wave of water erupted from the ground, crashing into the assassins with a brutal force. The ocean's fury had nothing on her now.

But even as the assassins were knocked back, they didn't fall. The leader, the tall one, rose from the ground, his eyes burning with fury.

"You think you can stop us, mage?" he spat. "You and your fire-loving friend are nothing but a nuisance."

Lyra's heart raced as she turned to Caelan. His flames flickered out for a moment, his focus shifting as the assassins regrouped, their eyes sharp and calculating. They weren't here to capture her—this was a hunt.

"We need to get out of here," she breathed.

But as the words left her lips, the storm intensified. Lightning cracked across the sky, a jagged flash of light that split the air in two. In that instant, the ground beneath them seemed to shudder, and Lyra's power surged uncontrollably. Water exploded from the cliffs, cascading down in a torrent that struck the assassins with the force of a tidal wave.

Caelan's fire reemerged with a flash, and together, they were a tempest—fire and water colliding, an unstoppable force. But Lyra knew this couldn't last forever. The assassins were relentless, and they were closing in fast.

"We have to go now," Caelan growled, his voice tight with urgency.

Without another word, they turned and ran, the storm at their backs and the assassins hot on their trail. The night was alive with danger, with fire and water waging war in a kingdom on the brink of destruction.

But even as they fled, Lyra couldn't shake the feeling that this was only the beginning.

The wind howled behind them, the storm now a full-on tempest, crashing with unrelenting fury against the cliffs of

Tidewell. Lyra's heart hammered in her chest as she sprinted, her feet barely touching the ground. Caelan was ahead of her, his fire illuminating the path as he created a wall of flames that forced their pursuers to fall back momentarily. But they couldn't afford to slow down—not with the assassins on their heels.

Each step felt like it carried them further into the heart of the storm, both literal and metaphorical. The lightning struck the ground with such violence that it seemed as though the sky itself was trying to tear apart. The ocean below roared with a deafening sound, and Lyra could feel the water surging beneath the earth, rising with every breath she took. She could almost taste the salt in the air, the scent of both fire and water mingling in a heady, dangerous cocktail.

Caelan's fire lit the path ahead of them, but Lyra could feel the strain in his movements. His flames were growing hotter, fiercer, as if he were fighting not just the assassins, but the storm itself. The world around them was becoming more unstable by the second, the earth trembling beneath their feet with each burst of power.

"Keep moving!" Caelan shouted over his shoulder, his voice barely audible over the roar of the storm. "They're closing in!"

Lyra gritted her teeth, her fingers curling into fists as she drew on the power within her. The water inside her surged again, but she kept it in check, forcing it back down. She couldn't lose control now—not when they were so close, not when their survival depended on it.

A sharp cry cut through the night air. One of the assassins had caught up, darting in from the side. With a flick of his wrist, a blade of silver gleamed in the moonlight. Lyra didn't see it coming until it was too late. He lunged.

But before the assassin could strike, Caelan whipped around, fire exploding from his palm in a violent arc. The flames roared through the air, searing the assassin's weapon into molten slag before it could reach Lyra. The assassin staggered back, his dark cloak singed and smoking, but still very much alive.

"We don't have time for this!" Caelan growled. His breath was ragged, his chest heaving from exertion. "We have to get to the forest. It's the only way."

The forest—the only safe place Lyra could think of, the last sanctuary between them and the Tidewell forces. They had to reach it, and fast. It wasn't far, but with the storm intensifying and the assassins getting closer, Lyra feared they might not make it.

Another assassin appeared to their right, more agile than the others, a blur of dark clothing as he lunged for Caelan. Lyra's heart lurched in her chest as she saw the assassin's blade glinting in the dim light. She couldn't let him reach Caelan.

She reached out, summoning the water once more. This time, there was no hesitation. She could feel it—deep within her, the power of the tide called to her. She willed the water to rise. It surged from the ground like a living thing, a great wave of water crashing down on the assassin with a violent force. He was swept off his feet, flung backward, and disappeared into the darkness.

Lyra took a step forward, only to stumble as the earth beneath her feet trembled again. The storm wasn't just a tempest in the sky. The very land seemed to shake, as if something deep below had been disturbed by their presence.

"We need to move, now!" she shouted, panic rising in her throat.

Caelan didn't need any more prompting. He grabbed her

arm, his grip tight but reassuring, and they both broke into a run again, the forest now within sight. The path grew steeper, the underbrush thick and tangled, but they didn't slow down. Every muscle in Lyra's legs screamed in protest, but she couldn't stop—not with their lives on the line.

Just as they reached the edge of the forest, the ground shook again, harder this time. A crack of thunder split the sky, followed by another bright flash of lightning. But in that moment, something else happened—something Lyra had feared but didn't want to acknowledge.

From the depths of the storm, something dark and powerful rose.

Caelan stopped abruptly, his eyes scanning the swirling darkness. Lyra felt it too, the shift in the air, the sudden tension that seemed to hang between them. The water, still restless within her, churned at the edges of her control. This wasn't just the storm anymore. There was something else—a presence, ancient and terrifying, that had awakened at the worst possible moment.

"Caelan," Lyra whispered, her voice thick with dread. "It's not just them… Something else is coming."

The earth trembled again, this time with a force so great that it nearly knocked them both to the ground. Caelan's fire flared up instinctively, the heat of it shooting out like a wave, but it was no match for what was happening. The storm roared louder, and in the center of the chaos, a figure emerged.

The figure was tall, cloaked in shadows, but there was no mistaking the power radiating from it. The storm bent around this figure, as if it were an extension of the man—or whatever he was. His eyes burned with a cold light, a supernatural gleam that sent a chill down Lyra's spine.

"The storm has come," the figure's voice rang out, its tone as cold and unfeeling as the wind itself. "And with it, the end."

Lyra's breath caught in her throat. This wasn't a normal assassin. This was something else entirely. Something far more dangerous. Something that seemed to belong to the storm itself.

"Who are you?" Caelan demanded, his voice steady despite the chaos around them.

The figure's lips curled into a faint smile. "I am the harbinger of what is to come. The one who will see the prophecy fulfilled."

Lyra's pulse raced. This was it. The prophecy—the one they had both tried to deny—was finally coming to fruition. The storm, the power growing inside her, the flame inside Caelan—they were all connected.

The figure raised his hand, and the storm responded. Lightning crackled across the sky, striking the ground near them with such force that the ground seemed to split open. The very earth was trembling beneath their feet, as if it were trying to swallow them whole.

"You cannot escape," the figure said, his voice echoing with a finality that chilled Lyra to her core. "This world is meant to burn, to drown. And you will be the ones to bring it about."

Caelan stepped forward, his fire burning brighter, hotter, a flash of light in the dark. "Not if I can stop it."

The figure didn't flinch. He simply raised his hand again, and the wind howled, the storm swirling around them in a violent cyclone. Lightning struck again, closer this time, and the force of it sent both Caelan and Lyra staggering back. The air was thick with energy, charged and alive with raw magic.

"We have to fight back!" Lyra shouted over the roar of the

storm, her voice barely audible.

She could feel the water growing stronger inside her, pushing against her chest, but she knew it wouldn't be enough. Not against this.

Caelan looked at her, his expression grim but resolute. "Together," he said.

And in that moment, with the storm closing in around them, Lyra finally understood what the prophecy meant. The flame and the tide—they had to unite. But it wouldn't come without a cost. It never did.

Lyra closed her eyes, drawing on the water, letting it rise within her, letting the ocean's power fill her. Caelan did the same, the fire in his chest crackling louder, roaring like a dragon ready to break free. They stood together, the very elements colliding, pushing against each other with such force that the ground beneath them groaned and trembled.

The storm screamed, the darkness closing in, and Lyra knew then that they were not just running from the assassins anymore. They were running from destiny. And it was coming for them, whether they were ready or not.

# Three

## Flame and Water

The wilderness of Tidewell was unforgiving.  It stretched out in every direction, a vast expanse of dense forests and towering cliffs that seemed to swallow the sky. The air was thick with humidity, the scent of wet earth and moss clinging to everything, while the distant sound of rushing water echoed like a constant reminder of the kingdom's power.

For Caelan, it was a land of contrasts—one where his flames felt out of place. The fire that had always been his ally, the element he wielded with such ease, now seemed weaker against the dampness in the air, as if the very atmosphere was working to stifle him. His clothes, still damp from the storm, clung to his skin, and the heat from his body couldn't fight off the chill that had crept into his bones. He glanced sideways at Lyra, her silhouette cutting through the mist like a figure made of water, and he couldn't help the ache that tugged at him. Her presence, though a constant source of tension, had become something else—something magnetic, something that both intrigued and terrified him.

They were traveling along a narrow path that led deeper into the forest, the trees towering above them like ancient sentinels. The storm had passed, but the remnants of it still lingered in the air. The wind was erratic, carrying the scent of the sea and the promise of something more dangerous. Every step they took seemed to draw them further into the heart of the wilderness, away from the threat of assassins but closer to an even darker destiny.

"You're not even trying to control it," Lyra's voice cut through the silence, her tone sharp with irritation.

Caelan glanced at her. She was walking a few paces ahead, her back stiff and her shoulders set in a way that betrayed her frustration. Her eyes were locked on the path ahead, but he could see the flicker of something more—something that burned between them, unspoken yet undeniably present.

"You think it's easy?" he shot back, his voice rough with the tension that had been building ever since they left the edge of the cliff. "This land… it doesn't welcome fire, Lyra. It's like the air itself is trying to drown me." He clenched his fists at his sides, willing the fire to remain contained, but the heat flared up anyway, making his skin burn. "And you think I'm not trying?"

She stopped and turned to face him, her eyes flashing with a fierce, untamed light. "You're not trying hard enough. I can feel it," she snapped. "You're letting it control you."

"I'm not letting anything control me," he retorted, stepping closer, his breath coming faster. "I'm doing the best I can. But you—" He cut himself off, his voice low and dangerous. "You think that water's going to save you. But it's the reason we're even here."

Lyra's jaw tightened, and her lips curled into a thin line. "I didn't ask for this either. I didn't ask to be bound to you by some ridiculous prophecy. But I'm trying, Caelan. I'm trying to help you. You're the one who's—"

"Who's what?" he interrupted, his voice rising with the heat that pulsed in his veins. "Who's what, Lyra?"

Her temper flared in response, her hands moving to her hips as she took a step closer to him. Her power, that cold, deep force, was palpable in the air between them, swirling around like the calm before a storm. She was dangerous, and for a brief, fleeting moment, Caelan considered stepping back. But something in him refused to. Something in him wanted the clash.

"Who's not listening to reason!" she finally spat, her words sharp. "You're so caught up in your damn fire that you can't see anything else!"

For a moment, the world stood still. The air crackled, as though the very atmosphere between them was charged with something neither of them could control. Caelan could feel the fire rising, hot and fierce, wanting to break free. His fists clenched, the flames curling at the edges of his fingertips, but he held it back. Just barely.

"Don't talk about my fire like it's a weakness," he growled, stepping closer to her, his chest tight with the sudden, overwhelming urge to break something. "This fire is the only thing that has kept me alive. It's the only thing I've ever been able to control."

Lyra's expression shifted, and she stepped back, her eyes hardening. "Then maybe it's time you learned to control something else," she said quietly, her voice colder than the water that surged beneath her skin.

Before he could respond, a sharp crack broke through the air, and both of them froze. The silence that followed was deafening. Then came the distant sound of something—someone—moving through the trees. They were not alone.

Lyra's eyes widened, her breath catching. "We're being followed."

Caelan's instincts kicked in. "We don't have time for this," he muttered, already reaching for his fire. But before he could unleash it, the unmistakable sound of approaching footsteps grew louder.

"No time for fire, either," Lyra said, her voice urgent. "We need to move."

Without waiting for a response, she grabbed Caelan's arm, pulling him toward a narrow opening in the forest ahead. He followed her, reluctantly dropping the flare of his fire, but not without a glance back. He could feel it—those watching eyes, lingering in the shadows.

The path ahead was steep and winding, the undergrowth thick and thorny. Lyra moved with ease, the water flowing like a current beneath her steps, leaving no trace of their presence as they hurried deeper into the forest. Caelan was slower, his every step heavier as the land seemed to fight him, the damp earth making his fire harder to sustain.

"We need to get to higher ground," Lyra muttered, her eyes scanning their surroundings. "We can't keep running forever."

Caelan nodded, his jaw clenched. "Agreed."

They continued up the steep slope, the forest growing thicker, the shadows longer. The air was heavy with moisture, the oppressive weight of the storm still clinging to the leaves above them. But as they climbed, Lyra's gaze suddenly shifted, her eyes narrowing as they swept over the trees.

"Something's ahead," she said, her voice low, cautious.

Caelan frowned. "What do you mean?"

"I can feel it," she said, holding up a hand, palm open to the air. "A current, pulling toward something."

He felt it too—the shift in the air, the hum of magic on the wind. It was subtle at first, but it grew stronger, more distinct. A whisper in the air. A call from somewhere deep in the wilderness.

Without a word, they both followed the sensation, pushing through the thick brush, until they reached a large rock formation. The path narrowed here, and the earth beneath them was slick and treacherous. Lyra paused at the base of the rocks, her eyes searching the surface.

"There," she whispered, pointing.

A hidden opening was barely visible in the side of the rock, a small crevice leading into darkness. Lyra moved first, stepping forward with confidence, as though she had known this place her whole life. Caelan hesitated for a moment before following her, his hand brushing the damp stone as they ventured into the narrow passage.

The air inside the cave was cool, the scent of earth and water mixing in a way that reminded him of the sea. It was quieter here, the sound of the forest muffled by the thick stone walls. Lyra led the way, her pace quick and sure. They wound through the cave, the passage twisting and turning as if it had a mind of its own.

Finally, they entered a large chamber. The walls were smooth, the air thick with magic, and in the center of the room stood an ancient altar, half covered by ivy and moss.

On top of it lay an object—a stone, smooth and black, with intricate carvings etched into its surface. Caelan could feel its power even from a distance, like a pulse under his skin.

Lyra stepped forward, her eyes fixed on the artifact. "This is it," she whispered.

Caelan frowned, his mind racing. "What is it?"

Lyra didn't answer immediately. She reached out, her fingers brushing against the surface of the stone. As soon as she touched it, the carvings on the artifact began to glow faintly, the symbols shifting and rearranging before his eyes.

"This is the key," she said softly, almost to herself. "The artifact of the ancients. It's said to hold the power to unite the elements, to stop the war before it begins."

Caelan's pulse quickened. "How do we use it?"

Lyra turned to face him, her eyes intense. "We don't know yet. But it's our only hope."

Just as she reached for the artifact again, a sharp sound echoed through the cave—a low, menacing growl.

They weren't alone.

From the shadows of the cave, dark figures began to emerge, their eyes gleaming with malice. They moved with a predatory grace, their movements too smooth, too deliberate to be human. Caelan's fire flared again, but Lyra held up her hand, stopping him.

"These are no ordinary assassins," she whispered. "They're something darker."

The figures advanced, their eyes locked on the artifact. And at that moment, Caelan realized that this was no accident. Someone—someone powerful—had been waiting for them. And now, it was too late to turn back.

The figures in the shadows shifted, and Caelan's instincts flared. His hand instinctively reached for the fire burning beneath his skin, but Lyra's calm voice stopped him before the flames could fully ignite.

"Don't," she whispered urgently, her expression one of both warning and understanding. Her hand was still outstretched toward the artifact, but her eyes were fixed on the approaching figures, her body tense with the recognition of a greater threat.

The dark figures emerged from the deeper shadows of the cave, their forms impossibly tall and cloaked in tattered black robes. Their faces were hidden, obscured by the hoods that shrouded them. But the air around them crackled with an unnatural energy, a darkness that seemed to bend the light itself. It wasn't just the assassins who had been following them—it was something else entirely.

Caelan felt the heat of his fire rise, instinctual, but it was suffocated by the oppressive energy that filled the cavern. The temperature seemed to drop, and a shiver ran down his spine.

"We need to leave," Lyra muttered under her breath, her eyes scanning the room for a possible escape. "This place is more dangerous than we thought."

The figures didn't move. They stood perfectly still, their presence commanding the very space they occupied, as if they were waiting for something. Caelan's fingers itched for his magic, but the pull of the water and the dark energy surrounding them seemed to twist the very air. It was as if both his fire and Lyra's water were being suppressed, rendered insignificant against the looming threat.

One of the figures, taller than the rest, stepped forward. His movements were unnervingly slow, deliberate, and yet his presence was suffocating. The air grew colder with each step he took, and the shadows around him seemed to deepen.

"You should not have come here," a voice, low and cold, emanated from beneath the figure's hood. The words sent a chill through Caelan's bones. It wasn't a voice that belonged to any human—it felt like the voice of the cave itself, ancient and predatory.

Lyra's grip on the artifact tightened. Her voice was firm but laced with the tension that only came from a deep, uncontrollable fear. "We don't want any trouble. We're not here to disturb what's been hidden for centuries."

The figure's hood shifted, and for a brief moment, a glint of golden eyes gleamed from the depths of shadow, their gaze piercing through the darkness. Caelan's heart skipped a beat as the figure's lips curled into an almost imperceptible smile.

"Disturbance?" the voice rasped, barely audible. "You are the disturbance. You, the fire mage and the water-bearer. You who dare to challenge the natural order."

Lyra's eyes flashed with a mix of defiance and caution. "We are only here for what was promised. The artifact—" She hesitated. "—is the key to preventing the war. We are not your enemy."

The figure stepped closer, his form growing darker, more insistent with each step. "You know not what you seek, water mage. The artifact is not for your kind. And the flames you carry are too dangerous to be set loose."

Caelan could feel the tension build, the fire roaring inside him, trying to break free. He fought to keep it contained, but the more the figure approached, the stronger the pull became. He glanced at Lyra, seeing the same struggle on her face. Her water, once calm and soothing, churned beneath her skin, restless and eager to react.

"We won't let you stand in our way," Caelan said, his voice filled with a mixture of warning and resolve. "Step aside, or we'll force our way through."

The figure didn't flinch. He raised his hand slowly, and in response, the shadows around them seemed to grow thicker, swirling, as though they were alive. The temperature dropped even further, biting at Caelan's exposed skin.

"You will not pass," the figure said, and his voice grew stronger, more commanding. "The artifact is not for mortals to wield. Its power is ancient, bound to forces beyond your comprehension. And you will not awaken that which sleeps."

Lyra's grip on the artifact tightened further. She stepped forward, her water magic swirling at her feet, and Caelan could see the flash of something deep within her—a spark of determination, of strength, that mirrored his own.

"You don't understand," Lyra said, her voice quiet but resolute. "The prophecy binds us. We have no choice but to see it through. The world is at stake, and we are the only ones who can stop it."

The figure's golden eyes flashed, and for the briefest moment, Caelan thought he saw something akin to a smirk beneath the hood. "The prophecy," he repeated. "Yes, the prophecy. But you fail to see the true cost of it. The fire and water… they are not meant to unite. That is not the way the world was made. It is an abomination."

Lyra's face paled at the figure's words, but she didn't retreat. "We don't care about what the world was made to be. We care about stopping what's coming."

Caelan stepped forward, his fire burning brighter with each heartbeat, a dangerous flare of power ready to break free. "If you stand in our way, we will burn everything that stands between us and the truth."

The figure's smile widened, and for a moment, the shadows around him seemed to writhe, as if alive. "Very well. If it is fire you wish, then fire you shall have."

The ground beneath them trembled as the figure raised his hand, and the shadows surged forward with a terrifying speed, stretching toward them like long, dark tendrils. Caelan reacted immediately, his fire bursting into life, a torrent of flames roaring from his palms. The air around them crackled with the sheer intensity of his magic, a violent clash of fire and shadow that illuminated the cave in blinding bursts.

Lyra reached out with her water magic, a surge of energy flooding the air as she called on the ocean's strength, but the shadows seemed to twist and pull at the water, dragging it back, dissipating her control.

"We can't fight this alone," Lyra shouted over the growing storm of shadows and fire. "Caelan, we have to work together. We can't let them stop us."

He could feel it—the pressure building, the opposing forces warring inside him. The shadows pushed back against his flames, the cold suffocating the fire, while Lyra's water struggled to keep the darkness at bay.

"Now!" Caelan shouted, a desperate edge to his voice.

He took a deep breath, forcing himself to focus, to center his magic. The fire inside him flared brighter, fueled by Lyra's call to action. They had to combine their powers—only together would they be strong enough to break through the barrier that the figure had created.

Lyra stepped forward, her eyes locking onto his. For a moment, the world seemed to still around them, the storm of shadow and fire halted by the intensity of their connection.

And then, together, they released everything.

The fire surged like a tidal wave, rushing forward and colliding with Lyra's water, merging into a single force. It was both overwhelming and beautiful—a cascade of flame and water intertwined, working together, each feeding off the other's strength. The shadows shrieked as they were engulfed, the darkness pushed back by the overwhelming surge of combined power.

For a moment, the cave was silent, the air thick with magic. But then, as the light from their combined power began to fade, Caelan felt something shift. The ground beneath them trembled again, but this time it was different. A new presence, darker and more malevolent, was coming.

The figure who had challenged them staggered back, his eyes wide with something Caelan couldn't identify—fear, perhaps, or disbelief. But before he could act, a deep rumble shook the cave, and the walls began to crack.

"Leave now," the figure hissed, his voice dark with a warning. "Before it's too late."

But it was already too late.

The earth split open beneath their feet, and a surge of water, laced with fire, tore through the cavern, sweeping the shadows aside and shattering the cave's defenses. The light from the artifact, still pulsing with power, flared brighter than ever, and Lyra, Caelan, and the figure were all consumed by the magic.

Outside the cave, the storm raged again, and the sound of it was deafening, a final warning of the chaos they had unleashed. They had only just begun to realize the true cost of their power, and the battle for the fate of the world had only just begun.

# Four

# A Shifting Alliance

The village of Varro's Hollow lay at the edge of the Great Divide, a forgotten settlement nestled between the warring territories of Emberfall and Tidewell. It had once been a thriving community, a place where fire and water, though at odds elsewhere, had lived in fragile peace. Now, it was a hushed ghost of its former self—its buildings half-destroyed, its streets empty, save for the occasional rebel fighter or weary traveler seeking refuge from the ever-encroaching chaos.

Caelan and Lyra arrived at dusk, the horizon stained with streaks of crimson and violet as the sun dipped behind the jagged cliffs of Emberfall. The air was thick with tension, a constant reminder of the simmering war just beyond the village's borders. The remnants of the storm still lingered in the atmosphere, its dark clouds pressing heavily upon the land, as though the storm had refused to leave until the world's turmoil had settled.

Caelan's boots crunched against the dry earth as he walked beside Lyra, their footsteps echoing in the silence. His eyes flicked constantly to the shadows around them, every rustle of wind, every faint movement, setting his nerves on edge. There was no mistaking the danger in the air—the village, though seemingly abandoned, was not safe.

"Are you sure this is the place?" Lyra asked, her voice calm, but with a hint of apprehension. She could feel the unease rolling off Caelan, the sharp edge of his tension that matched the storm brewing in his heart.

He glanced at her, his face taut with unspoken words. "This is the last stop before we reach the resistance's safe house. If they're as good as the rumors say, we'll be safe here for a while. But after that, we'll need to keep moving."

Lyra nodded, though her thoughts were a tangle of doubts. Safety was a fleeting illusion in their world. She had seen it in the way the storm clouds gathered around them, felt it in the way the fire inside Caelan always threatened to combust. They were two opposing forces, brought together by something neither of them fully understood. But for now, she was content to trust in him, even if that trust was a fragile thing.

The village was eerily quiet. A handful of figures moved in the distance, but they kept their distance, their faces hidden behind hoods or masks. Caelan tensed every time one of them glanced their way, his hand hovering near his belt, where his dagger lay.

As they made their way through the narrow streets, they were led by a silent figure—a man with a scarred face and a weathered cloak that marked him as a member of the resistance. His name was Thorne, and his eyes were as sharp as the knife he carried. He led them through the heart of the village, weaving through alleyways and crumbling buildings until they arrived at a hidden door set into the side of an old, abandoned tavern.

Thorne knocked twice, then once more, a rhythmic pattern that seemed to match the pulse of the world around them. The door creaked open, and they were ushered inside by a woman with dark, piercing eyes and a scarred hand that bore the mark of the rebellion.

"Welcome," she said, her voice cool but not unfriendly. "You must be the fire mage and the water-bearer. We've been expecting you."

Caelan's hand tightened into a fist, but he forced himself to relax. "You know us?"

"We've had our eyes on you for some time," she replied, stepping aside to allow them entry. "The prophecy, the artifact… it hasn't gone unnoticed."

Lyra glanced at Caelan, her brow furrowing. "What prophecy?"

The woman studied her for a moment before answering, her gaze assessing. "The one that binds fire and water together. The one that says you're the only ones who can prevent the war between the kingdoms. We know the risks, the danger that surrounds you both."

Lyra's heart skipped a beat. The resistance knew about the prophecy? The very prophecy that had only recently begun to take shape in their lives? She shot a look at Caelan, whose jaw was clenched tight, his fire simmering just beneath the surface.

"We didn't come here to be a part of your rebellion," Caelan growled, his voice low, tinged with frustration. "We came for refuge, not to be dragged into another war."

The woman's eyes hardened slightly. "You misunderstand, fire mage. We're not asking you to join our cause. We simply wish to offer you shelter from the storm that's coming."

Lyra stepped forward, her calm presence immediately tempering Caelan's heated reaction. "We appreciate your help," she said, her voice steady. "But we have our own path to follow."

The woman regarded her silently for a moment before nodding. "I understand. But you'll find that the path you walk will soon cross with ours. The world is shifting, and there are those who would see both of you dead before you can fulfill your part in the prophecy."

The tension in the room thickened as the weight of her words settled between them. The door behind them creaked, and a young man stepped into the dimly lit room. His eyes flicked over Caelan and Lyra with a calculated glance, and his posture was relaxed, yet purposeful. He had the air of someone who was both dangerous and intelligent, and Lyra didn't trust him immediately.

"This is Aric," the woman said. "He's one of our leaders. He's been tracking your movements for days now."

Aric stepped forward, his hand outstretched in a gesture that was almost too casual. "Welcome to the Hollow," he said with a faint, sardonic smile. "I imagine your journey's been a long one. It'll be good to have you here, even if only for a short while."

Caelan didn't move to shake his hand. His eyes narrowed, and his body remained tense. "I don't trust you."

Aric's smile faltered slightly, but he didn't react with anger. Instead, he seemed amused. "Wise. But I assure you, we're not your enemy."

Lyra stepped between them, her voice calm but firm. "We're not looking for trouble. We just need to rest, to regroup."

Thorne motioned for them to follow him, and they were led down a narrow hallway to a small room with a low, wooden table and a handful of chairs. The walls were lined with maps, some of which were too old to be of any use, others marked with recent scribbles and notes. Lyra could feel the air heavy with the weight of the rebellion, the desperation of those who had been fighting for far too long.

As Thorne handed them a map of the surrounding area, he spoke in hushed tones. "The monarchy of Tidewell has spies everywhere, even in the heart of Emberfall. We can't trust anyone who isn't part of our cause."

Lyra glanced at Caelan, her hand instinctively resting at her side. The fire within him was restless, a constant hum beneath his skin. The rebellion's plans, their cause—she didn't know if it was worth it. They had enough to contend with already without becoming pawns in someone else's game.

But Caelan's voice cut through the silence. "What exactly do you want from us?" he asked, his voice low but filled with barely-contained anger. "We're already caught between two kingdoms at war. Why drag us into this?"

Thorne's eyes met his, unblinking. "Because we need your help. The kingdoms are preparing for all-out war, but there's something we can do. There's an artifact buried deep in the mountains, one that holds the power to unite the kingdoms— or destroy them. We need you to find it before anyone else does."

Lyra felt a chill creep up her spine. She had heard whispers of such an artifact, but this… this was different. The artifact was said to be a powerful force, one that could tip the scales in the war—if it fell into the wrong hands.

"I'm not doing this for you," Caelan spat, his anger flaring. "We're here to survive, not play your games."

Lyra placed a hand on his arm, her calm presence forcing him to look at her. She could feel the fire within him burning too hot, too fierce, and she knew that he wasn't thinking clearly. His temper had always been his greatest weakness, the one thing that could throw him off balance.

"We'll help," she said, her voice steady. "But we do it on our terms."

Caelan shot her a look, his eyes blazing with frustration. "You're going to trust them?"

Lyra met his gaze, her expression softening. "We don't have a choice."

But just as she finished speaking, the door to the room slammed open with a force that sent the chairs clattering to the floor. A man staggered in, his face pale and his breath coming in short, panicked gasps.

"They're coming!" he shouted, his eyes wide with terror. "The Tidewell soldiers! They've found us!"

The room exploded into chaos as rebels scrambled to arm themselves. Lyra's heart pounded in her chest as she turned to Caelan, who had already moved into position, his flames crackling to life.

"They'll be here any minute," Aric said, his voice sharp with urgency. "We need to move, now."

Caelan shot a look at Lyra, his temper bubbling to the surface. "What now? Run and hide?"

Lyra's calm presence steadied him. "We don't run," she said quietly. "We fight."

And as the sound of footsteps grew louder, closer, the air

heavy with the weight of betrayal and danger, Caelan and Lyra found themselves facing the greatest test yet—whether to trust the shifting alliance they had been pulled into or face the storm alone.

The tension in the room snapped like the taut string of a bow, and before anyone could speak another word, the door was slammed open again. This time, a group of armed men stood in the doorway, their faces grim and hardened, their eyes scanning the room with ruthless efficiency. They were soldiers, and from the looks of it, not the kind who took prisoners.

Lyra felt the blood drain from her face. The Tidewell soldiers were here, their presence unmistakable. The chill in the air deepened, and she could almost feel the weight of their magic— cold, cutting, and unforgiving. They had found them. The village, the safe house, everything was compromised.

"We've been betrayed," Thorne muttered under his breath, his hand instinctively going to the hilt of his blade. The others in the room immediately tensed, each one preparing for the inevitable clash. But the soldiers didn't move immediately. They stood there, a barrier between the rebels and the only exit.

Lyra could hear her own heartbeat thundering in her ears, but she refused to give in to the panic threatening to claw its way up her throat. Caelan's fire was already rising—she could feel the heat from across the room. It was a dangerous thing, but it was also their only hope.

The leader of the soldiers stepped forward, his face sharp with a cruel, knowing smile. He had the look of someone who relished in control, in power. His eyes fixed on Caelan and Lyra.

"Well, well," the man said, his voice smooth, mocking. "The fire mage and the water-bearer. I see we've found you, after all."

Lyra's jaw clenched. She stood tall, trying to match his gaze, but she could feel Caelan beside her, his anger almost palpable, radiating off him in waves. She placed a hand on his arm, trying to steady him. She needed him calm—needed both of them to keep their heads if they were going to get out of this alive.

"You know," the leader continued, eyeing them both with an almost predatory curiosity, "I had wondered just how long it would take for you two to show up. The prophecy, the artifact… you're more trouble than you're worth. But you'll make a fine sacrifice for the greater good, don't you think?"

Caelan's fire flared up in response, his hands suddenly ablaze with crackling energy. "You think you can just take us?" His voice was a low growl, thick with fury. "You've underestimated us."

Lyra could feel his rage—the flame inside him was struggling to break free. The heat that poured off him was intense, and it was tempting to let it burn, to let him release the fury inside him. But she knew what would happen if they both lost control. She had to keep him grounded.

"Caelan," she whispered, her voice as calm as she could manage. "Control it. We need to get out of here, not burn it all down."

But before he could respond, the leader raised his hand, a signal, and the soldiers moved in unison. They spread out, their swords glinting in the dim light, blocking all exits. Lyra's pulse quickened, and she could feel the water inside her, restless and ready to defend them. But there was no time to prepare.

"We don't need to fight," the soldier leader said, his smile widening. "We just need you to come with us. The Tidewell monarchy has plans for you, and they don't take kindly to resistance."

Lyra's mind raced. She had to think. This wasn't just a battle of magic—it was a battle of wills. And they had no choice but to outwit them.

"Plans?" she repeated, her voice steady, though inside, her thoughts were racing. "What plans?"

The leader's grin faltered slightly, but only for a moment. "The kind that ends with the world being reshaped. The artifact you seek—it's ours. And you will be the ones to unlock its true power. All we need is your cooperation."

Lyra's eyes flicked to Caelan, whose fire still burned dangerously close to the surface. She knew he wouldn't stand down, not with the soldiers so close. Not with the pressure building between them. She had to make a decision—stay and fight, or make a break for it and trust they could find a way out.

"We won't cooperate with the monarchy," Lyra said firmly, her voice steady as she took a step forward. "The artifact isn't yours to control. And neither are we."

The soldier leader's eyes flashed, a sharp glint of anger behind his cold exterior. "Stubborn," he hissed. "Fine. You can choose to die here, or you can come with us. Either way, the prophecy will be fulfilled."

In that moment, the air between them seemed to snap, as if the weight of the world was ready to collapse in on itself. Caelan was shaking with barely-contained fury. His magic crackled in the room, burning brighter with every passing second. He was ready to lash out, to burn everything to the ground. But Lyra, even with the overwhelming presence of the soldiers, knew they needed a plan. They couldn't just rely on sheer power.

"Move," she whispered urgently, a soft but deliberate command in Caelan's ear.

He hesitated, his fiery eyes burning into hers. She could see the conflict in him, the desire to unleash his power, to obliterate them all. But she was his anchor. Her calmness, her focus, pulled him back, just enough to let the heat simmer instead of erupt.

"Now," she urged.

Before the soldiers could make their next move, she called on the water. The air around her seemed to hum with the magic that rushed to her command. In a flash, a blast of water shot from the floor, slamming into the nearest soldier and knocking him off balance. The others reacted too slowly, the sudden surge of water enough to momentarily disorient them.

Lyra seized the opportunity. She grabbed Caelan's arm and yanked him toward the narrow hallway behind them. "Go!" she shouted, and together, they bolted, their steps echoing in the tight corridor.

Caelan's fire flared once more, lighting their path as they pushed through the twisting hallways of the safe house. Behind them, the sound of shouting soldiers grew louder, their footsteps quickening as they scrambled to regain control. Lyra could feel the weight of the danger pressing down on them, the very air thick with urgency. They had to move fast, or they would be cornered.

The tunnel ahead led to an exit, a hidden door that opened into a dense forest beyond the village. The night was cold, but it wasn't the chill of the wind that made her shiver—it was the realization that they were not safe, not anymore.

They reached the exit, just as the soldiers' shouts echoed behind them. Lyra pushed the door open, feeling the cool night air rush in like a breath of fresh air. But just as she stepped through, Caelan grabbed her wrist, stopping her. His face was tight with frustration, his eyes wild with fury.

"They'll follow us. They won't stop until we're dead," he muttered, his voice thick with rage.

Lyra could see the fire in him, flickering and restless, but it wasn't enough. They couldn't fight their way out of this. Not yet. Not with the entire resistance under threat.

"We can't outrun them. We have to trust the plan," she said, her voice steady but firm. "We need to get to the mountains. That's where the artifact is hidden. We can't let them take it."

Caelan's eyes softened, just for a moment, as he realized the truth of her words. They couldn't keep running forever. But they also couldn't afford to fail. Not now.

"Alright," he muttered, his voice low and resigned. "But we're not playing their game. We'll find a way to win this, together."

The words hung in the air as they moved swiftly into the night, disappearing into the dark woods, their connection growing stronger with every step, even as the danger surrounding them threatened to pull them apart.

Behind them, the soldiers began to regroup. The hunt was on, and they would stop at nothing to capture Caelan and Lyra. But the fire and water, bound together, were far more dangerous than anyone realized.

And soon, the storm would break.

# Five

## Flames of Betrayal

The night was thick with silence, a heavy fog that curled through the trees of the forest like a living thing. Caelan and Lyra, along with a small group of resistance fighters, moved cautiously through the dense undergrowth, the rustling of leaves the only sound accompanying their swift, careful steps. The tension in the air was palpable. The escape from the village had been barely a step ahead of the Tidewell soldiers, and every move they made now felt like a calculated risk, one misstep away from disaster.

"Keep moving," Thorne whispered from ahead, his voice low and urgent. He led the way, his eyes flicking constantly to the shadows behind them. "We're not safe yet. The forces in these woods are too well-positioned."

Caelan's eyes narrowed, his senses heightened. He could feel the weight of the night pressing in on them, an oppressive presence that seemed to follow them with every step. His fire simmered just below the surface, restless, but he knew better than to let it flare up too soon. They were too close to danger.

Lyra walked beside him, her footsteps silent, her senses equally alert. She could feel the water, the distant hum of it buried deep within the earth, calling to her, urging her to tap into it. But she resisted, knowing that it was too risky to let her power grow too wild. The very magic that could save them could just as easily destroy them, especially if it were to spiral out of control.

The resistance had led them to this forest, a place of refuge they had hoped would offer some reprieve. The path they walked was hidden, a web of forgotten trails designed to protect them from the enemy's eyes. But Lyra knew it wouldn't be long before their enemies found them. And Caelan… Caelan's temper was becoming harder to control. She could feel it—his frustration, his doubts, all of it building like a storm on the horizon.

The trees closed in around them, and the faint sound of rushing water from a nearby river seemed to grow louder with each step. They were drawing closer to their destination, a safe house where they would meet with the rest of the rebel forces. But it didn't feel like safety. It felt like the calm before a storm.

And then, like a crack of thunder, the ambush came.

A sudden noise broke the stillness—a rustling in the underbrush, followed by a low growl. Before anyone could react, a line of soldiers emerged from the shadows, their movements swift and fluid. They were too many to fight off, too well-armed to escape. Caelan barely had time to draw his blade before they struck.

The forest erupted into chaos. A volley of arrows flew

through the trees, cutting the air with a deadly precision. Caelan and Lyra fought back instinctively, but they were outnumbered. Soldiers charged from every direction, their eyes cold, merciless. The resistance fighters scattered, trying to regroup, but it was clear that this was no ordinary skirmish. This was an ambush, a trap set specifically for them.

Caelan's fire blazed to life in an instant. He swung his sword, sending a trail of fire crashing through the air, setting the trees alight. The flames roared, but they didn't stop the soldiers. They pushed forward, relentless, forcing Caelan and the others back. Lyra's water responded, but it was a slow, measured effort. She summoned the water from the nearby river, but the soldiers were closing in too fast.

The battle raged on, the forest a blur of flames and water, of steel and desperation. Caelan moved with a brutal grace, cutting down enemies left and right, but with each strike, he felt the fire inside him burn hotter, more uncontrollable. He could feel his power pushing him, urging him to go further, to unleash everything. He fought the urge, but the tension in his chest grew with every swing, every blow.

And then it happened.

In the middle of a fierce clash, Caelan's fire flared uncontrollably, an explosion of heat and light that tore through the air. It wasn't just a flame—it was a force, a violent eruption that sent soldiers flying in every direction. The trees around them caught fire in an instant, the flames crawling up the trunks like tendrils of a living beast.

Lyra screamed.

The explosion had caught her off guard. She had been too close to Caelan when the magic erupted, and the force of the blast threw her backward, crashing into the ground with a sickening thud. Her head slammed against the dirt, the world spinning in a blur of heat and smoke. Her vision blurred, her body aching from the impact. She tried to push herself up, but everything felt wrong, her limbs too heavy, her breath too shallow.

"Lyra!" Caelan's voice broke through the haze, desperate and filled with panic. He dropped to his knees beside her, his hands shaking as he gently cupped her face. "Lyra, please. Don't—don't do this."

She could barely hear him, the ringing in her ears too loud, the pain in her head too much to ignore. But she tried to focus, tried to make sense of the world around her. Caelan's face loomed above her, his expression twisted in agony. His fire, now contained but still smoldering beneath the surface, flickered in his eyes.

"I—I'm fine," she whispered, her voice barely audible. "Just… just give me a moment."

But it was clear that she wasn't fine. The explosion had taken its toll on her. Her heart was pounding in her chest, and every breath was a struggle. The world was spinning around her, and all she could see was Caelan's face, filled with guilt, with fear.

"Don't lie to me," he said softly, his voice shaking. "I almost killed you."

She reached up, her hand trembling as she touched his arm. "You didn't mean to. It was an accident."

But Caelan didn't seem to hear her. His hand tightened around her, his fire flickering, his magic still too unstable to contain. He was on the verge of losing control again, and Lyra could feel the weight of it pressing down on them both.

"You almost killed me," he repeated, his voice rough. "I can't lose you."

"I'm here," she whispered, forcing herself to focus, to stay awake, to reassure him that she was still there. "I'm still here."

The fire within Caelan's eyes flickered uncertainly, the glow dimming for just a moment as he took a shaky breath. But before he could speak again, a voice called out to them from the edge of the clearing.

"Caelan! Lyra! We need to move!"

It was Thorne. He was standing just beyond the smoke and flames, his eyes wide with urgency. A small group of rebels had managed to regroup, but they were being overwhelmed. There was no time to linger.

Caelan's grip on Lyra loosened, but his eyes remained fixed on her. "Can you stand?"

Lyra nodded, though every movement felt like it took all her strength. "I can. But we need to move, Caelan."

He helped her to her feet, his hands gentle but firm. The world around them was chaos—fire and smoke filled the air, and the cries of battle echoed through the trees. Caelan's fire burned low now, the surge of power that had nearly killed her waning. But Lyra could feel the strain in his body, the toll it was taking on him.

"We can't stay here," Thorne called again. "They're closing in."

Caelan's eyes flicked to Lyra, his face drawn, the weight of the situation settling in. He didn't want to leave her, not like this. But they had no choice. They couldn't fight this battle, not here, not now.

"Go," Lyra urged, her voice stronger now. "We have to keep moving."

And so, they did. Caelan took her hand, his fire still

simmering beneath the surface, and they ran. They ran through the forest, the flames behind them licking at the trees, the sounds of battle fading into the distance. Every step they took brought them further from the chaos, but Lyra could feel the weight of the betrayal, the feeling that the prophecy they had been bound to was more than just a promise—it was a curse.

The bond between her and Caelan had been forged in fire and water, but now, as they fled for their lives, she wondered: was it fate that had brought them together, or had it simply been the cruel hand of destiny, forcing them into a war neither of them had chosen?

As they reached the edge of the forest, the first light of dawn broke through the trees, casting a golden hue over the landscape. But even the beauty of the new day couldn't wash away the doubt that lingered between them.

"We have to keep going," Lyra said quietly, her voice steady despite the storm of thoughts racing through her mind. "We're not done yet."

Caelan looked at her, his eyes full of pain, but also something else—something deeper. He nodded, though the guilt still weighed heavily on him. "We'll finish this," he promised, his voice low, filled with resolve.

But as they walked into the uncertain future, the question that hung in the air remained unanswered. Would they be able to control their magic—control themselves—long enough to stop the war? Or was the prophecy simply a trap, designed to tear them apart?

The bond between them, once so certain, now felt fragile, like a thread that could snap at any moment. But for better or worse, it was the only thing they had left to hold onto.

And as the sun rose higher in the sky, the flames of betrayal were not the only things they had to face.

The forest was eerily quiet as they moved further into the heart of the wilderness. The sounds of battle had long since faded, but Lyra could still hear the rushing of her own blood in her ears. Every step she took felt heavier than the last, and though she kept moving, part of her wanted to collapse, to sink into the ground and let the world spin around her.

Caelan, too, was on edge. His hand remained tightly wound around hers, his grip possessive and desperate. The bond between them was palpable, crackling in the air like a storm waiting to break. But Lyra could feel the tension beneath it— the doubts, the guilt, the unspoken fears that still hung between them like an invisible barrier.

They were silent for the most part, the only sounds their footsteps crunching over the forest floor, the occasional crack of a branch, and the distant call of some wild creature. It felt like they were the last two people alive in a world that had already burned itself to the ground.

Caelan finally broke the silence, his voice rough with unspoken emotion. "I almost killed you, Lyra. I don't know what happened. The fire just… it took over."

She glanced at him, her gaze soft but firm. "It wasn't your fault. You didn't mean to."

"I know," he muttered. "But that doesn't change what happened. I lost control. I could have killed you."

Her heart clenched at the pain in his voice. She could see it now—the struggle he faced every day, the weight of his own power, the constant battle between the fire that gave him strength and the fear that it would one day consume him.

"You're not alone in this," she said softly, squeezing his hand. "We're in this together. We've always been."

Caelan's eyes flicked to hers, a mixture of gratitude and fear in his gaze. For a moment, it seemed as though he would say something, something that would reveal the depth of his turmoil. But instead, he just nodded, his expression hardening again.

Ahead of them, Thorne's figure appeared from between the trees, his face grim. He held up a hand, signaling for them to stop. Lyra and Caelan halted immediately, their eyes searching the woods, looking for any sign of danger.

"What is it?" Lyra asked, her voice tense.

"There's a clearing up ahead," Thorne said, lowering his voice. "We're not alone. We need to move cautiously."

Caelan's hand tightened around Lyra's, and she could feel his pulse racing through their linked fingers. His instincts were sharp—he knew something was coming. She could sense it too, the unmistakable presence of someone—or something—just beyond the trees.

They fell into a tense silence, the weight of the unknown pressing down on them. Each step felt like it carried them closer to something inevitable, something they couldn't escape. Lyra tried to steady her breathing, but the fear was a gnawing presence at the back of her mind. Was it the Tidewell soldiers again? Or was it something worse?

They reached the clearing cautiously, the moonlight filtering through the trees and casting long shadows across the ground. Lyra's heart skipped a beat when she saw them.

The figures were cloaked in darkness, their faces hidden beneath hoods, their movements as silent as death itself. They stood in a loose circle around the clearing, their eyes glowing with an unnatural light. Their presence was unmistakable—the mark of the Veil of the Forsaken.

Lyra's breath caught in her throat. The Veil. The very dark society that had been pulling the strings of the world for centuries. The same group that had manipulated Caelan's fate, the one that had set the prophecy in motion.

She turned to Caelan, but he was already ahead of her, his fire flaring to life with a violent force. His magic surged through him, a powerful force that lit up the clearing with an eerie glow. The Veil members didn't move, didn't flinch. They simply watched, their cold eyes fixed on the pair of them.

"I thought we had lost you," one of the figures said, their voice a chilling whisper in the night. "But here you are, still alive, still defying the fate we've set for you."

Lyra felt a jolt of fear shoot through her. The figure's words echoed in her mind—the Veil had been waiting for them. This was no coincidence.

"Stay back," Caelan growled, his voice low and dangerous. His fire roared in response to his words, flaring higher, hotter. But the Veil did not move. Instead, they stood silently, waiting.

"Do you really think you can control it?" another figure spoke, stepping forward. Their face was shrouded in shadows, but the voice was unmistakable—it was Ivor, the warlord who had been hunting them.

Lyra's blood ran cold. She had heard of Ivor—his reputation was feared across both Emberfall and Tidewell. A ruthless leader, one who sought to control both fire and water for his own purposes. He was the very person they had been trying to avoid, the one who could change the course of the war.

"I've been looking for you," Ivor said, his voice cold, calculating. "And now, here you are, standing in front of me. The fire mage and the water-bearer. The prophecy will be fulfilled, whether you like it or not."

Caelan's fire burned brighter at his words, his eyes flashing with raw fury. "You won't control us, Ivor. We won't let you."

Ivor's laugh was low, mocking. "You don't have a choice. The prophecy binds you both. You've already done what was needed, whether you realize it or not. Now, you'll fulfill your part in the prophecy… or die trying."

Lyra stepped forward, her hand instinctively going to her side where the water magic thrummed beneath her skin. She could feel the tension in the air, the pull of the power that surged from both sides. It was overwhelming—fire and water, two forces vying for control. But she didn't hesitate. She couldn't afford to.

"We won't bow to you," Lyra said, her voice steady despite the growing sense of dread. "We'll stop you."

Ivor's gaze hardened, and in that moment, Lyra saw the true darkness within him. "You think you have a choice? You've been playing into our hands from the very beginning. The artifact is not for you. It's mine."

With a sudden motion, he raised his hand, and the ground beneath them trembled. The air was thick with an unnatural energy, and Lyra could feel it—the pressure building, the weight of the world shifting beneath their feet. She could barely react before the attack came.

The Veil members moved with terrifying precision. They raised their hands, and a dark force lashed out, striking Caelan with a blast of shadowy energy that sent him flying backward. The force of the strike was like nothing Lyra had ever felt. It was as if the very air had been torn apart.

"No!" Lyra screamed, rushing to Caelan's side as he hit

the ground, his body slamming into the dirt. His fire flared instinctively, but it was weakened, struggling to rise against the power of the Veil.

"Caelan, get up!" Lyra cried, her voice frantic. She reached for him, her water magic flaring to life as she tried to push back the dark energy that clung to him. But it was like trying to fight against a storm.

Caelan's eyes fluttered open, and for a moment, he just stared at her, disoriented. "Lyra… I can't… it's too strong…"

The doubt that had been creeping up on them both for days began to swirl inside her. Was this the end? Had they been wrong to believe in the prophecy? Had they been led here only to be destroyed by forces they could never control?

But she didn't have time to think. Ivor's voice cut through the fog of uncertainty.

"Run, if you want to," Ivor called, his voice dripping with malice. "But you can't escape what's coming. This is your destiny, and no one—least of all you—can change it."

Lyra's heart raced as she turned to look at Caelan, who was slowly trying to sit up, his body still trembling with the force of the blast. She reached for him, her fingers trembling. She could feel it—the bond that still held them together, despite everything.

"No," she whispered, her voice filled with resolve. "We won't run. We'll fight, together."

Caelan's gaze met hers, his eyes filled with a mix of fury and something softer, something deeper. He nodded, his fire reigniting, though it was a flickering flame. It wasn't enough yet.

But together, they were stronger.

Lyra summoned her water, pushing it outward in a tidal

wave that crashed into the Veil's dark magic, sending them stumbling back.  Caelan's flames surged in response, the heat rising once more, pushing against the shadows that surrounded them.

But even as they fought, the weight of Ivor's words lingered in the air, the question still gnawing at them both. Was the prophecy their salvation—or their undoing?

The storm was far from over, and the flames of betrayal burned hotter than ever.

# Six

# The Heart of the Storm

The wind howled through the trees like a living creature, its sharp bite slicing through the air. The storm had come from nowhere—one minute, the skies had been a muted gray, the air thick with tension, and then in an instant, the heavens had torn open, unleashing a fury that seemed to match the anger brewing between Caelan and Lyra.

Lyra could feel it now, the storm within her. The storm without. The two forces were one, clashing in a violent symphony of wind and water, fire and fury. Every gust of wind carried with it the faint scent of salt from the sea, but beneath it, there was something else—something darker, something far older. The power that had once been a part of her family, a power that had been taken from them long ago.

She stood on the edge of the cliff, the violent winds whipping her hair around her face, her cloak fluttering like a dark flag in the tempest. Below her, the sea raged, its waves crashing against the jagged rocks far below. The waves were enormous now, taller than any she'd ever seen, their white caps frothing like the ocean itself was being torn apart.

Beside her, Caelan was a living storm in his own right, the heat of his flames rising against the wind, yet they seemed to fight each other, a battle between fire and water. His figure was a dark silhouette, his body tense, the fire around him dancing wildly. But even as his power flared, she could feel the weight of the storm pushing at him too. His magic was bound to hers in ways neither of them fully understood.

They had been running for days now, ever since the ambush by Ivor's soldiers, pushing forward, trying to escape the ever-encroaching darkness. But the storm had found them anyway. This was no ordinary storm—it was something much deeper, much darker. The sea, the wind, the very earth beneath them were all rebelling against something. It was as if the storm was waiting for them, as if it had been summoned, just like they had been.

"You need to stop," Lyra shouted, her voice almost lost in the wind. She turned to Caelan, her eyes locking onto his with a desperation she hadn't felt before. "You're making it worse."

"I can't just let it rage!" Caelan's voice was strained, thick with the effort of holding back the flames that licked the air around them. The fire around him crackled like the sound of a thousand sparks, bright and untamed. He was fighting the storm, trying to keep his flames under control, but the power of the wind and the water seemed to push at him, force him to release everything.

"Caelan, please," Lyra pleaded, stepping closer to him, feeling the heat of his fire burning against the freezing wind. "We're feeding it. The more you fight, the stronger it gets."

He turned to her, his face a mask of frustration and determination, his brow furrowed, his jaw tight. "I don't know what else to do! This... this storm is *our* storm, Lyra. It's born from us, from what we are. You feel it, don't you?"

She nodded, though the admission cut at her. She had felt it—the storm inside her, the power of the sea and the earth, the same power that had once been her family's legacy. The power that had been stripped from them when her family was betrayed, cast aside by those they had once trusted. The power that had burned them all to the ground, leaving only ashes behind.

"I know," she said, her voice softer now. She reached out, her hand brushing his arm, feeling the heat of his magic under her fingers, the fire that was both dangerous and alive. "But we have to learn to control it. We have to work together, Caelan. If we don't—"

The words died on her tongue as a violent gust of wind tore through the air, flinging her backward. The force of it knocked the breath from her lungs, and she stumbled, her feet sliding against the slick, wet ground. She reached out instinctively, but her fingers couldn't find purchase, and she was falling, falling into the abyss.

"Lyra!" Caelan's voice rang out, full of panic. His flames erupted again, and in the next instant, he was beside her, grabbing her arm, pulling her back to solid ground. His flames blazed around them, but the wind howled against him, pushing at the fire, keeping it from reaching its full potential.

Lyra gasped for breath, her heart racing as she looked up into his eyes. They were full of fear, of a wild, desperate energy. He had saved her, but the storm was still here, relentless, pounding against them.

"I told you," she said, her voice breathless, her hands shaking. "This storm is ours. We've been summoned into it, whether we want to be or not. We're tied to it, Caelan. And it's not just the weather—it's everything. My family's magic, my betrayal, everything is tied into this."

Caelan's face softened, his gaze flicking to the raging sea below them. "Your family," he murmured, his voice tinged with both understanding and sadness. "They betrayed you?"

Lyra swallowed, her throat tight. She turned away from him, looking out over the dark waters, her mind racing. "My family were water mages, the most powerful in all of Tidewell. We were revered, feared. But... but the monarchy saw us as a threat, saw our magic as something to control. My parents— they were betrayed by those they trusted the most. By their own people."

Her voice wavered, and she had to swallow the lump in her throat. The memories were sharp, too painful to revisit, but they needed to understand each other. They needed to be whole in this—together.

"The monarchy exiled us," she continued, her eyes distant, lost in the past. "My parents were murdered. I was left to survive on my own. I couldn't stop them, couldn't stop what they did. And the worst part is... I'm the last of us. The last of the water mages."

The wind howled, the waves below crashing violently against the rocks, as though the earth itself was mourning with her. Caelan stepped closer, his hand gently resting on her shoulder, his touch a grounding force in the madness of the storm.

"I didn't know," he whispered, his voice soft. "I had no idea,

Lyra. I thought your magic was just something you could control. But it's more than that. It's a part of you—your family, your history. And this storm… it's not just about us. It's about everything we've lost."

She nodded, the tears she hadn't allowed herself to shed threatening to spill. But she refused to cry—not in front of him. Not when there was so much at stake.

"I'm not the only one who's been betrayed," Caelan said after a moment, his voice steady, though there was a flicker of pain behind his words. "My family—they used me, too. They've always used me, made me believe I was their weapon, their heir to a throne that I never wanted. I was just a tool in their war."

Lyra turned to look at him, her heart aching at the vulnerability in his eyes. "You're not a weapon," she said fiercely, her hand gripping his. "You're not anyone's tool."

The fire in his eyes flickered, not with anger this time, but with something deeper—something softer. "You make me believe that," he said quietly.

The storm around them raged on, but in that moment, in the eye of it all, there was peace between them. The bond they shared, the connection forged in fire and water, was undeniable. And for a brief moment, Lyra believed they could control it all. Together.

But then, as if the heavens themselves had decided to test them, the storm surged, the winds intensifying, the waves rising higher, crashing against the cliffs with a deafening roar. Lyra felt the water within her stir, restless, pulling at her, calling to her in a way she couldn't resist.

"No," she whispered, panic creeping into her voice. "We need to stop it. We need to control it."

Caelan's flames burned brighter, his magic responding to her urgency. "We can't—there's too much. It's too big."

But she didn't listen. She reached out, extending her hands toward the sea, toward the storm, willing it to calm, to quiet. The water surged in response, rising higher, but it wasn't enough. The storm didn't stop—it grew stronger, more insistent, as though the world itself was fighting them, pulling them deeper into its heart.

"Caelan, help me!" Lyra cried out, desperation in her voice.

Caelan's fire surged, intertwining with her water, but the two forces collided violently, sending shockwaves through the air. The storm intensified, the winds howling like a living beast. The earth beneath their feet trembled, and Lyra felt the cold grip of fear in her chest.

They were both too powerful, too volatile. Fire and water, bound together, were like two forces meant to destroy each other, and they had no control.

But in the midst of it all, something shifted between them. Lyra felt it—her connection with Caelan, the strength of their bond, the love that had begun to blossom between them. And with that love, she found the clarity she needed.

"Focus," she said, her voice low but firm. "Focus on me, Caelan. We're stronger together. We control this."

He looked at her, his eyes filled with uncertainty, but he nodded. His fire began to dance with her water, the two forces now working in harmony, not against each other. The flames softened, and the water receded, swirling around them in a delicate balance.

The storm didn't stop, but it slowed. The winds lessened, the waves calmed. The world began to settle, as if the earth was taking a deep breath after a long, violent struggle.

And in that moment, as they stood there, their magic intertwined, Lyra knew something she hadn't before. She and Caelan weren't just two opposing forces—they were the key to something greater, something that could bring the world back from the brink of destruction. Together, they could tame the storm. Together, they could control everything.

But as the storm subsided and the first rays of dawn began to break through the clouds, Lyra knew that their journey was far from over. The path ahead was uncertain, but one thing was clear: no matter what came next, they would face it together.

And nothing, not even the fury of the storm, could tear them apart.

The storm began to fade, the winds gradually losing their intensity, the violent clash of water and fire subsiding into a quiet, uneasy calm. The moon, once hidden behind thick, swirling clouds, began to peek out from behind the remnants of the storm, casting an eerie, pale light over the landscape. The sea, still churning beneath them, seemed to soften, its waves no longer crashing violently against the cliffs but moving in a more rhythmic, controlled pattern, as though acknowledging the balance that had just been restored.

Caelan and Lyra stood amidst the aftermath, their breathing labored, their bodies sore from the strain of battling both the storm and their own powers. The air around them crackled with residual energy, the magic that had been released still lingering in the atmosphere, palpable and alive.

Caelan's fire was no longer burning bright, but it still simmered beneath his skin, just barely contained. Lyra could feel her water, the pull of it, calling to her from deep within. But neither of them let their powers surge again. They were both exhausted, their bodies spent from the force they had used to calm the storm.

Lyra wiped her brow, feeling the cool remnants of the mist that lingered from the storm settling on her skin. Her heart was still racing, but it wasn't fear that gripped her anymore. It was something else—something deeper. She turned to Caelan, her eyes meeting his.

For a long moment, neither of them spoke. They stood there, the world around them still recovering, and Lyra could feel the unspoken weight of everything that had passed between them. The betrayal of their families, the prophecy that had bound them together, and the uncertainty of the future—all of it was here, between them, hanging in the air.

"I can't believe we did it," Caelan said finally, his voice rough, but soft. He turned to her, his expression a mixture of disbelief and wonder. "We actually controlled it. The storm… it was ours. We did that."

Lyra nodded, the words catching in her throat. "Together," she added quietly, her voice almost a whisper.

He looked at her for a moment, his eyes searching hers, as if trying to read her thoughts, trying to understand what had just happened. His gaze softened, the fierce fire in his eyes now tempered with something gentler.

But then, as if to break the moment, a gust of wind suddenly picked up, swirling around them once more. It wasn't as violent as before, but it was enough to remind them that their magic was still a volatile force, not something to be recklessly wielded.

Lyra turned her face into the wind, her hair whipping around her face. The storm had passed, but the echoes of its power lingered. The storm outside was over, but the storm inside her heart raged still, untamed and unpredictable.

"What happens now?" she asked softly, though she wasn't sure if she was asking him, or the universe itself.

Caelan hesitated, his hand brushing against hers in a brief touch, a soft reassurance. "I don't know," he admitted. "We've come this far, but the road ahead... it's still a mystery. We've made enemies, Lyra. Ivor, the Veil, the kingdoms. They all want us. They want what we can do."

Lyra closed her eyes, taking a steadying breath. He was right. Their enemies were closing in, and every moment they spent together seemed to draw the world's attention closer. She could feel the weight of their shared destiny pressing down on her chest, the uncertainty of their future as heavy as the storm clouds that had hung over them just moments before.

But despite the fear and the doubt, despite everything, there was something inside her that refused to break. The bond between them, the fire and the water, wasn't just about power. It was about something more. Something deeper.

"I'm not afraid," she said, her voice barely above a whisper, but it was steady, strong. "We've already come this far. I'm not turning back. No matter what happens, Caelan... I trust you."

His eyes softened again, his gaze locking onto hers, and for a moment, everything else seemed to fade away. The storm, the enemies, the uncertainty—it all disappeared as he looked at her, his expression vulnerable, raw.

"I trust you too," he murmured, his voice rough, yet filled with a quiet intensity. "We'll face whatever comes together. We have to. I don't know if I can do this without you, Lyra."

The air between them seemed to shift then, as if their combined powers, their magic, had drawn them closer than ever before. She could feel the fire within him, the heat that had once terrified her, now tempered by her own water. They were not opposites—they were two sides of the same coin, two forces that needed each other to exist.

Before she could respond, the sound of footsteps echoed from behind them, snapping them both out of their reverie. Lyra's pulse quickened, and she turned, instinctively drawing back, her magic pulsing beneath her skin in response to the sudden shift in the air.

Caelan, too, immediately braced himself, his fire flaring up again in preparation. His gaze shot to Lyra, and for a moment, they were both poised on the edge, ready to fight, ready to face whatever danger lay ahead.

But it wasn't an enemy that approached.

Thorne emerged from the trees, his face grim, his expression more serious than Lyra had ever seen it. Behind him, a small group of rebels followed, their eyes wary, their faces set with determination.

"Caelan, Lyra," Thorne called, his voice low but urgent. "We've got trouble."

Lyra felt her heart tighten in her chest. She could see the tension in Thorne's eyes, the anxiety that laced his every word. Whatever was coming, it was far worse than she had anticipated.

"What is it?" Caelan asked, his fire flickering in response to the unease that began to settle over them both.

Thorne didn't answer immediately. Instead, he glanced over his shoulder, as if making sure no one was following them. He lowered his voice. "We've received word—an army is on its way. Ivor's forces, and some of his allies, are closing in on us. They know where we are."

Lyra's stomach sank. The storm, the battle, the enemy's

relentless pursuit—it was all coming to a head. And they were running out of time.

"How long?" Caelan asked, his voice hardening with the weight of their situation.

"A few hours," Thorne replied. "They've been tracking us. They've been waiting for the right moment. And now, they have it."

Lyra's heart raced as the words sank in. She turned to Caelan, her hand reaching for his, her fingers curling around his wrist. "We can't run anymore, can we?"

"No," Caelan said quietly, his voice resolute. "We won't run. But we can't fight them all head-on, not yet."

"We'll have to outsmart them," Thorne said, his tone grim. "We've set a trap of our own, but we need to move fast. We need to get to the mountains before they do. If we don't, it's over."

The realization hit her then, hard and fast. The path ahead of them was not just about survival. It was about making choices—choices that would determine the fate of the world, of everything they had fought for.

The prophecy. The artifact. And now, Ivor and the Veil.

But there was one thing that was clear—she and Caelan had made it this far because they had each other. The storm had tested them, torn them apart, but it had also bound them together in ways neither of them could have predicted.

"You're right," she said, her voice steady, though her heart was still racing. "We'll face this. Together."

Caelan's gaze softened as he looked at her, his expression both weary and resolute. He reached out, his hand brushing hers gently, the warmth of his touch grounding her in the chaos.

"Together," he whispered, his voice a promise, a vow.

As the storm finally began to die down around them, the quiet after the chaos seemed almost unnatural, like the calm before something far worse. The world around them was still torn by war, by betrayal, by the power they could barely control. But for the first time in what felt like forever, Lyra allowed herself to believe, if only for a moment, that they could overcome whatever came next.

They would face the storm together.

And nothing, not even the darkest of betrayals, would tear them apart.

## Seven

# The Tides of War

❦

The silence was deafening.

Caelan and Lyra stood on the cliff's edge, watching as the first light of dawn broke through the darkened skies, casting an ethereal glow over the lands stretching out before them. The once calm sea now churned with waves too high, too violent. The air was thick with tension, both from the brewing storm and from the storm between the kingdoms of Emberfall and Tidewell, which had been escalating for days. A sense of inevitability hung in the air—like the calm before a battle, before a storm that would consume everything in its path.

Far below, the waters crashed against the jagged rocks, the spray rising into the air like white-hot fury. Lyra could feel it, the water's restless pulse, mirroring her own growing unease. The power within her had been surging for days, growing stronger and harder to control. It was as if something inside her was waking—an ancient power that had been dormant for far too long.

"Do you feel it?" she asked, her voice barely a whisper.

Caelan turned his head, his fiery gaze meeting hers. There was something in his eyes, something hard and determined. His fire still simmered beneath his skin, restless and hungry, like it had been for weeks now. He could feel it too—the tension, the pull between them and the world that was ready to break.

"I feel it," he said, his voice low, strained. "It's like we're on the edge of something... something dangerous."

Lyra nodded, her heart pounding in her chest. The closer they got to the heart of the prophecy, the more intense the connection between them became. But it wasn't just their bond that worried her. It was what the prophecy meant for the future of both their kingdoms. If they revealed it, would their people accept them? Or would they become the very thing the kingdoms feared? Would they become the catalyst for the war they had tried so desperately to avoid?

The weight of the decision pressed on her like a physical force, one that she could barely escape. If they revealed the truth of the prophecy, it could ignite a firestorm that neither of them were ready to face. If they kept it hidden, they risked being torn apart by the kingdoms' warring factions.

"I can't keep running from this," she murmured. "The prophecy—it's everything. And nothing. It's both a promise and a curse."

Caelan's eyes softened, but there was a shadow behind them, a flicker of doubt. He took a step toward her, the heat from his body pushing against the cool air of the morning. "We don't know what this means yet, Lyra. The prophecy, our connection—everything is shifting. And if we make the wrong choice, everything we've worked for could burn."

Lyra looked out over the sea, feeling the pulse of her power beneath her skin, the water calling to her. "It's already burning, Caelan. I can feel it. I can feel the world breaking, the kingdoms teetering on the edge of war. And my magic… it's growing. It's becoming harder to control. If we can't figure this out soon, I'm afraid I'll lose myself."

The words hung in the air between them, heavy with truth. The water had always been her ally, but now it was overwhelming, pulling her in ways that felt both intoxicating and terrifying. The magic that flowed through her was ancient, tied to the heart of the world itself, but as her powers grew, so did the danger of losing herself to them. She had seen it in the eyes of her ancestors—the look of those who had let the power consume them.

"We have to decide, Lyra," Caelan said, his voice a rasp, filled with quiet urgency. "We can't keep running. The prophecy will catch up to us, whether we like it or not. The kingdoms are already at war. The longer we wait, the more lives will be lost."

She closed her eyes, the weight of his words sinking deep into her chest. There was no escaping this. No running. The battle between fire and water was coming. It was inevitable. But they still had a choice—how to face it, and what role they would play in the coming storm.

"I can't make this decision alone," she said, turning to face him. "I need you, Caelan. We need each other, not just for our magic, but for our hearts. I need to know… can we trust what we feel for each other? Or is it just another lie, another trick of fate?"

Caelan looked at her, his gaze searching, burning with something deeper than the fire that raged within him. He reached out, his hand brushing against hers, the heat of his touch grounding her, anchoring her to the moment.

"We have no choice but to trust," he said softly, his voice full of quiet resolve. "I've felt it, Lyra. The pull, the connection between us—it's real. And whatever the prophecy means, whatever it's supposed to bring, I believe we can face it. Together."

Her heart skipped a beat at his words. She had known, deep down, that they were bound together, not just by the prophecy, but by something more. It was more than just their powers—it was the fire and water within them, two forces that had always been at odds, yet somehow were made to coexist.

But there was still doubt. There was still fear.

Before she could respond, the ground beneath them trembled, the very earth vibrating with an intense power. Lyra's heart stuttered in her chest as she turned toward Caelan, her hand instinctively reaching for him. The storm, the magic that raged around them, was not just the weather. It was a reflection of what they were becoming.

The sea below rose in a violent swell, and the wind howled louder, pushing against them with a force that threatened to tear them apart. It was as though the very earth was rebelling, responding to the chaotic energy that pulsed from Lyra's magic and Caelan's flames.

"Lyra!" Caelan shouted, his voice barely audible over the roar of the storm. "We have to control it! Now!"

She looked at him, her pulse quickening. She could feel the power within her, the water threatening to burst free, to rage like a tidal wave. Her body ached from the strain of holding it back, but she knew she couldn't afford to let it go. Not yet.

"I can't hold it much longer!" she cried, her voice strained. "The water—it's too much!"

Caelan moved closer to her, his fire flaring up in an attempt to balance the power, but the storm intensified, the magic between them clashing. The wind tore at them, howling like a living beast, and the waves below crashed higher, the sea growing more violent with every second. The prophecy had warned them of this—their powers together were a force that could either save or destroy the world. And now, standing in the heart of the storm, they were forced to decide if they were ready to bear that weight.

"Lyra, we can't do this alone!" Caelan shouted over the storm. "We need to work together. You have to trust me."

She turned to him, her heart racing. She could see the fire in his eyes—the same fire that had consumed him, that had drawn them together. But it was more than that now. It was the trust they had built, the connection that had been forged in the heart of their shared magic.

"I trust you," she said, her voice a whisper, but filled with conviction.

In that moment, everything shifted. The storm around them seemed to quiet, if only for a heartbeat, as their magic intertwined. Lyra called on the water, pulling it from the depths, but this time, it was different. She wasn't just controlling it. She was guiding it, letting it merge with Caelan's fire, finding the balance they had both been seeking.

Caelan's flames swirled around her, not in opposition, but in harmony. The heat of his fire fused with the cold of her water, creating something new, something neither of them had anticipated. It wasn't just fire and water. It was something greater, something that had been waiting for them to realize.

Together, they could control it.

The storm that had threatened to consume them began to calm, the waves subsiding, the wind slowing. The energy that had been swirling between them began to settle, the storm quieting in the wake of their combined power. They stood together, their hands clasped, their magic still thrumming beneath their skin, but no longer threatening to tear them apart.

But the quiet that followed was just as intense as the storm itself. They were not out of danger yet. The kingdoms were still on the brink of war. The prophecy was still out there, and they still didn't know what it would bring. But for the first time, Lyra allowed herself to believe in the possibility that they could face it together.

"We can't turn back now," she said softly, her voice filled with determination.

"No," Caelan agreed, his gaze steady and sure. "We face this together. No matter what comes."

They stood there, the weight of the world on their shoulders, the storm at their backs, and the future uncertain before them. But the bond between them was undeniable, and in that moment, it was all they needed.

Together, they would face the heart of the storm.

And whatever it brought, they would survive it.

The quiet that settled around them felt fragile, like the calm after a tempest, where every breath was measured, every heartbeat too loud. Caelan and Lyra stood at the edge of the cliff, the faintest remnants of the storm still echoing in the distant sea. The once violent waves had receded, now nothing more than gentle ripples, their anger spent for the moment. The wind had died down, but the air was thick with the aftershocks of the power they had just unleashed.

Lyra stood still, her hands trembling at her sides, though she couldn't quite tell if it was from the strain of her magic or the emotions that churned within her. The water that had once surged beneath her skin, threatening to overwhelm her, now pulsed with a strange calm, as if it had found its balance—at least for now.

Caelan's fire was still present, though much subdued. It simmered beneath his skin like the coals of a dying fire, steady and contained. The flames had burned brighter and fiercer than she had ever seen them before, and for a moment, she had feared they would consume him entirely. But now, they had settled, a controlled force in his body that seemed to resonate with her own magic, in a way that felt almost… right.

"We did it," Lyra whispered, though the words felt inadequate for the magnitude of what they had just experienced. She glanced at Caelan, her eyes searching his face for any sign of doubt or fear, but there was none. He looked back at her with a quiet resolve that mirrored her own.

Caelan's lips quirked into a faint smile. "For now, anyway," he said, his voice rough but tinged with something else— something softer, something that made her heart beat faster despite the heaviness of everything they had just faced.

"I still don't know what this means," Lyra admitted, her voice faltering for just a moment as she looked out over the horizon, the land and sea merging into a seamless expanse of uncertainty. "For us. For the kingdoms. For the prophecy."

"We don't have to have all the answers right now," Caelan said, his voice steady, but the weight of his words settled between them like a solid truth. "But we know one thing—we're not facing it alone. And I trust you."

Her heart fluttered at his words, the sincerity behind them making her chest tighten. She turned to face him fully, stepping a little closer. "I trust you too," she said, her voice quiet but filled with something deeper than just words. It was a promise, an understanding that had been forged between them in the fires of their shared journey.

The sky above them was beginning to clear, the first rays of dawn casting a soft golden light across the landscape. The storm had passed, but the scars of it remained, like the aftermath of a battle fought within the heart of the world itself.

"Do you think it's over?" she asked, her voice filled with uncertainty.

Caelan shook his head. "No, not yet. The kingdoms are still on the brink of war. The prophecy still looms over us, and the forces that would use it to destroy us are still out there."

Lyra nodded, her thoughts racing. She knew that the peace they had just fought to achieve was fragile. The prophecy—the one that had bound them together—was still a secret. And with it, the uncertainty of whether they would be able to control their combined powers. Whether they could truly stop the war that was brewing.

But there was something else, something that she hadn't fully admitted to herself. The deeper connection between them—stronger than just fire and water—was the greatest risk of all. Could they trust their feelings? Was this love between them truly a force for good, or was it another part of the prophecy that they couldn't control?

The thought lingered in her mind, but she pushed it away, not yet ready to face it. Not yet ready to let that uncertainty consume her.

Before she could speak again, a shout echoed from behind them, pulling her from her thoughts.

"Lyra! Caelan!" Thorne's voice rang out, urgent and filled with tension.

Lyra turned, her hand instinctively reaching for Caelan's, and together they stepped away from the edge of the cliff, moving quickly toward the sound of Thorne's voice. The rebels had been moving in the shadows since their escape from Ivor's forces, and Lyra had known that the peace they had just found would be short-lived.

Thorne emerged from the trees, his face grim, his eyes wide with something she couldn't quite read. Behind him, several other rebels, including Aric, followed closely, their faces tight with worry.

"What's happened?" Caelan demanded, his voice laced with urgency.

Thorne didn't waste any time with pleasantries. "They're coming," he said, his voice low. "Ivor's forces. The armies of both kingdoms. They're already marching toward the capital."

Lyra's stomach dropped. She had known it was coming, but hearing it out loud felt like a punch to the gut.

"Already?" she asked, her voice barely above a whisper.

Thorne nodded grimly. "The rebellion is weak, but they've made their move. And now, the monarchies are preparing for full-scale war. It's happening faster than we anticipated."

Caelan's fists clenched, the fire inside him flaring in response to the news. Lyra could feel the heat from him, but it wasn't directed at her—not this time. It was directed outward, at the injustice of it all.

"We have to stop this," he said, his voice firm. "We can't let them destroy everything. The prophecy—our powers—this is what we've been preparing for. We can't back down."

Thorne stepped closer, his face serious. "We need to decide, Lyra, Caelan. The kingdoms won't wait for us to make a choice. Ivor's armies are on the move. We need to either reveal the prophecy now—unite the fire and water—or we keep it a secret and hope we can use it to our advantage."

Lyra turned to Caelan, her heart racing. She could feel the weight of the decision pressing on her. If they revealed the prophecy, it would either unite the kingdoms—or tear them apart. It could change everything, but could they truly control the power they had just unlocked?

"I don't know if we can trust the people of either kingdom," she said, her voice quiet, though there was a strength in her words. "There's too much hate, too much division. Even if we reveal the truth, can we make them believe us? Can we make them understand that we're not enemies?"

Caelan's eyes softened as he looked at her, his hand reaching out to take hers, grounding her in the midst of the chaos. "I don't know," he admitted, his voice tinged with frustration. "But we have to try. We can't keep running from this. We have to be the ones to bring them together, or we'll all be consumed by it."

Lyra nodded, the fire of determination lighting within her chest. She felt the weight of the choice, the burden of the future, but there was something else too—a sense of clarity. She knew what they had to do. They had to reveal the prophecy, even if it meant risking everything. Even if it meant facing the wrath of both kingdoms.

"We'll do it," Lyra said, her voice filled with quiet resolve. "We'll tell them. But we'll need to act quickly. If we don't, Ivor and his forces will destroy any chance we have at peace."

Caelan's expression softened, and for a moment, it was just the two of them, standing together in the quiet aftermath of the storm. But the moment passed quickly, as it always did, and the weight of the decision settled back into place.

"We'll do it together," Caelan said, his voice steady. "We face this, Lyra, side by side. We bring the kingdoms together, or we tear them apart."

Thorne looked between them, his eyes calculating, and then he nodded. "We'll need help," he said. "We can't do this alone. But I'll stand with you."

"Me too," Aric said, stepping forward. His face was hard, his eyes unwavering. "I'll stand with you, no matter the cost."

The rebels, though weary and battle-worn, stood resolute. Their loyalty was evident in their eyes, in their posture. The fight was far from over, but for the first time, Lyra felt a glimmer of hope. She wasn't alone in this.

"Then let's make our move," she said, her voice quiet but filled with resolve. "We have no time to waste."

As the group began to move, preparing for the next stage of their journey, Lyra couldn't help but feel the weight of what lay ahead. The kingdoms were on the verge of war, and the power within her, within Caelan, was the key to everything. The prophecy—what it meant for their world—still loomed large, but as they stepped into the unknown, Lyra allowed herself to believe that maybe, just maybe, they could change the course of destiny.

Together.

# Eight

## The Ember's Dilemma

The air in Emberfall was thick with smoke, the pungent scent of burning wood lingering long after the fires had been extinguished. Caelan stood on the balcony of the castle, gazing out over the kingdom he had once called home. The city sprawled below him, the fires of the previous battle still smoldering in the distance. The kingdom of Emberfall, a place built on fire, on strength and power, now stood at the edge of a precipice. The conflict between his kingdom and Tidewell was a ticking bomb, ready to explode at any moment.

But it wasn't just the war that weighed on him. It was the prophecy, the ancient words that had bound him and Lyra together, and the impossible choice that lay ahead. He had always thought of himself as a soldier, loyal to Emberfall, loyal to his family, his duty. But now, as the flames of war grew closer, he found himself questioning everything he had ever known.

"Caelan." The voice that called his name broke through his thoughts, and he turned to see Orin standing behind him. His childhood friend, his closest companion, had changed over the years, his face harder, his eyes colder. Orin had always been a man of discipline, of loyalty to Emberfall, but now, there was a shadow behind his gaze. The fire that burned in his heart had been tempered by the harsh realities of war. And it wasn't just the kingdom that had shaped him. Orin had his own ambitions now—ambitions that, Caelan feared, could pull them apart.

"You've been out here for hours," Orin said, stepping closer. "The war won't wait for you to brood over the past."

Caelan turned fully to face him, feeling the weight of his old friend's presence like a physical force. The fire in Orin's eyes was unmistakable, a fire that Caelan had once shared, but now felt so distant. Orin wasn't the same man he had known. His hands were rougher, his posture more rigid. The soldier who had once laughed and fought beside him was now a general in Emberfall's army, a man of war and bloodshed.

"I'm not brooding," Caelan replied, his voice low. "I'm thinking. I have decisions to make, Orin."

Orin's eyes narrowed slightly, but his expression remained unchanged. "Decisions, huh? Like the one you've been avoiding for weeks?" He stepped closer, his gaze unrelenting. "The prophecy, Caelan. You've been dancing around it long enough. You know what it means. You know what it could mean for Emberfall."

Caelan flinched at the words, feeling the weight of them pressing down on him. The prophecy. The one that had been foretold since ancient times. It had brought him and Lyra together, two forces—fire and water—meant to either unite the kingdoms or tear them apart. It was a prophecy that had brought nothing but chaos, and Caelan had never wanted any part of it. But now, it seemed like the only path forward.

"I know what it means," Caelan said quietly. "But what if it's a trap, Orin? What if we're being led to destruction?"

Orin's jaw tightened, his gaze hardening with frustration. "That's what I'm trying to tell you, Caelan. It's a trap. This whole prophecy is nothing but a tool, a weapon meant to weaken Emberfall. You've been blinded by it. By *her*."

Lyra's name hung between them like a challenge, like an accusation. Caelan's chest tightened, but he held Orin's gaze, unyielding.

"You don't understand," Caelan said, his voice rising slightly, as the old anger from their years of friendship crept back into his words. "I *do* understand. I understand that I can't just ignore it. I understand that Lyra and I—" He stopped himself, his breath catching in his throat.

Orin stepped closer, his tone sharp. "Lyra? You think that's why you're doing this? Because of *her*? You're forgetting who you are, Caelan. You're forgetting your duty. You're forgetting Emberfall, your family, everything we've worked for."

The words stung, each one sharper than the last. Caelan had always known where Orin's loyalty lay, but hearing it said so plainly, as if his own loyalty was in question, twisted something inside him.

"I haven't forgotten anything," Caelan said, his voice dangerously low. "But what if Emberfall has been wrong all along? What if the prophecy isn't just about fire and water? What if it's about something else? Something neither of us understands?"

Orin's face hardened, and for the first time in a long while, Caelan saw a flicker of doubt in his eyes. But it was fleeting.

The general inside Orin was quick to take hold again.

"This is about power, Caelan. You know it as well as I do," Orin said, his voice now ice-cold. "Tidewell has always been a threat. And now, with your prophecy—*our* prophecy, you're playing right into their hands."

Caelan's chest tightened at Orin's words. He wanted to believe that this was just a misunderstanding, that Orin hadn't changed so much. But deep down, he knew that things had already changed—had been changing for months, ever since the storm that had begun this journey.

"You think I'm playing into their hands?" Caelan's voice was almost a whisper now, raw with frustration. "I don't know what to think anymore, Orin. I don't know who to trust."

Orin's eyes softened for just a moment, and Caelan could see the old friendship that had once been there, buried under layers of time and war. But it was fleeting. The moment passed, and Orin stepped back, his eyes narrowing again.

"I don't want to fight you, Caelan. But if you side with her—if you side with the prophecy—you'll have to choose. Emberfall or her. You can't have both."

The words hit Caelan like a blow to the chest. He had always known that this day would come, but hearing it spoken aloud, hearing the finality in Orin's voice, made it real.

He turned away, the weight of the decision pressing down on him like a thousand tons of stone. The air was thick with heat, but Caelan felt cold. Every fiber of his being screamed to follow his duty, to side with Emberfall. It was everything he had known. It was everything he had been taught to fight for.

But Lyra… Lyra was the other half of the prophecy, the water to his fire. She had changed him. She had made him see that the world was not as simple as the black-and-white divisions he had grown up with. She had made him question everything he had been taught to believe.

"I don't know if I can make this choice," Caelan whispered to the wind, the words lost in the chaos of his heart.

Orin's voice, low and resolute, came from behind him. "Then you're already lost."

Caelan turned slowly, meeting Orin's eyes once more. The general's gaze was hard, unyielding, and for the first time, Caelan realized the true depth of their divide. Orin had become a symbol of everything Caelan had once been—a soldier, a loyal son of Emberfall, ready to fight for his kingdom no matter the cost.

But Caelan was no longer that man. He wasn't sure who he was anymore, but he knew one thing for certain: He couldn't turn his back on Lyra. He couldn't ignore the connection they shared, the bond that had been forged in the heat of fire and water. It was something ancient, something that went beyond the prophecy, beyond Emberfall or Tidewell.

"I won't betray her, Orin," Caelan said, his voice firm, his resolve settling like the weight of the earth beneath his feet. "I won't betray myself."

Orin's eyes flared with anger, his fists clenching at his sides. "Then you're a fool, Caelan. And when the kingdom falls, when everything we've built crumbles under the weight of your *feelings*, remember this moment. Remember who tried to stop you."

Caelan felt the sting of Orin's words, but he didn't flinch. "I'll face the consequences," he said quietly. "But not with you, Orin."

Without waiting for a response, Caelan turned away and began walking toward the entrance of the castle, his heart pounding in his chest. He knew that this was the point of no return. He had chosen his path, and it would not be an easy one.

As he stepped into the cold air outside, the weight of his decision hit him like a wave, but it was a wave he had already started to ride. He had chosen Lyra. He had chosen love, chosen the unknown, chosen the future that lay ahead of them.

And no matter what came next, no matter how much Emberfall—or anyone else—tried to tear them apart, Caelan knew one thing for certain: He would face it with Lyra by his side.

The storm was far from over. But for the first time in his life, Caelan didn't feel like he was running from it. He was ready to face it head-on. And he would face it with Lyra, no matter the cost.

The cold wind bit at Caelan's skin as he moved through the castle's courtyard, each step heavy with the weight of the decision he had just made. He barely registered the sounds of the soldiers training nearby, their shouts and the clash of steel on steel muted by the thundering beat of his heart. The castle, once a place of comfort, now felt alien to him. The familiar stone walls, the banners that hung proudly, seemed oppressive, closing in on him like the walls of a cage. He had left the world he had once known, and there was no turning back now.

As he passed through the castle gates, the open space beyond seemed almost infinite, yet it felt more suffocating than any room he had been in. The storm had passed, but in its wake, the air was thick with anticipation, the kind of anticipation one feels before the inevitable clash. His future, his destiny, was on a razor's edge. One wrong move, and everything would fall apart.

And yet, in the midst of it all, there was Lyra. Her face, her touch, her voice—everything about her had become his anchor in the storm. He had made his choice, but the burden of it, the consequences of turning his back on Emberfall and everything he had known, pressed down on him with an intensity that threatened to crush him.

The weight of Orin's words still lingered in his mind, echoing like a dark refrain. *When the kingdom falls, when everything we've built crumbles under the weight of your feelings...*

His jaw clenched. He couldn't afford to let those words fester, not now. There was too much at stake, and he had already decided. There was no turning back.

He made his way toward the stables, his thoughts drifting to Lyra. He had to find her. They needed to talk. They needed to solidify their bond, to prepare for what was coming. It wasn't just Emberfall and Tidewell anymore—it was everything. It was the prophecy that had brought them together, the very force that was both their salvation and their undoing.

Caelan was so lost in his thoughts that he didn't hear the footsteps behind him until it was too late.

"Caelan."

The voice came like a blade cutting through the stillness. He turned sharply, his heart leaping into his throat. There, standing just a few feet away, was Orin. His expression was a mix of anger and frustration, but there was something else behind his eyes—something more calculating, more dangerous than Caelan had seen before.

Orin crossed his arms, his gaze unwavering. "I knew you'd leave. I knew you'd turn your back on everything. But I didn't think you'd be foolish enough to throw it all away for her."

Caelan's fists clenched at his sides, the fire that had simmered in his chest flaring back to life. "I haven't thrown anything away, Orin. I'm making a choice—my choice. And it's not yours to question."

Orin stepped closer, his eyes narrowing as he looked Caelan up and down. "You think this is just about you and her? You think this is just some fantasy you're chasing? This is about the kingdom, Caelan. This is about *your* kingdom. This is about our people, our future."

Caelan's breath caught in his throat, the sting of betrayal cutting deeper than he had anticipated. "You don't get it, Orin. This *is* about our people. It's about what's best for Emberfall. And right now, I think the best thing for Emberfall is for us to stop fighting each other."

Orin's face hardened, his jaw tight with barely-contained fury. "You've always been soft. You've always wanted to believe in some idealistic dream. But out here, in the real world, dreams don't win wars. *We* win wars. With strength. With loyalty. With fire. You've forgotten that."

Caelan felt a sharp pang of regret at the words, but he refused to back down. He had seen the truth now. The kingdom he had once served had never truly been a place of honor or fairness. It was a kingdom built on oppression, on fear. And Caelan had been too blind to see it until now.

"You've changed," Caelan said, his voice cold, devoid of the warmth that had once marked their friendship. "I'm not the one who's changed, Orin. You have."

Orin's gaze flickered briefly, but then his anger flared brighter, his stance becoming even more rigid, more authoritative. "You think you're the hero here? You think you're the one who gets to decide what's best for Emberfall? You've been played, Caelan. You've been manipulated by the very people you're trying to save."

Caelan's heart thudded painfully in his chest as he took a step toward Orin. "What are you talking about?" he demanded.

"The prophecy," Orin spat, his voice low and venomous. "It's a lie, Caelan. A trap. They've been using you, just like they've used everyone before you. This—" He pointed to Caelan and then to the distant horizon, as if encompassing the entire world. "—is a game. And you're just a pawn in it."

Caelan's pulse quickened. His throat tightened with the weight of Orin's words, and for a moment, doubt began to creep in, like a creeping shadow across his thoughts. Was it possible? Had he really been played?

"No," Caelan whispered, more to himself than to Orin. "No. I refuse to believe that. I can't believe that."

Orin's face twisted into a grimace, his expression hardening even further. "You'll see the truth soon enough. When this war begins, when everything falls apart, you'll realize just how wrong you are. And you'll regret ever choosing her."

The words cut deeper than Caelan had expected. He looked at Orin, seeing only a stranger now—someone who had been consumed by the very things Caelan had once held dear. There was no trace of the boy he had known. Orin had become just another soldier in a kingdom that thrived on war.

"I won't let you turn me against her," Caelan said, his voice steady despite the turmoil rising within him. "I won't let you use the prophecy to tear us apart. You can't take this from me."

Orin's eyes darkened, and for a moment, it was as if he was considering something. Then, he took a deep breath and exhaled slowly, his shoulders dropping slightly. "I'm trying to save you, Caelan. I'm trying to save Emberfall. But if you won't listen, if you won't see the truth, then I guess there's nothing left to say."

The cold finality in Orin's voice made Caelan's chest tighten. But he didn't flinch. He wouldn't.

"I'm done with this," Caelan said, turning on his heel, walking away from his old friend without another word.

Behind him, Orin's voice followed him, quieter now but filled with a deadly resolve. "You'll come back to us, Caelan. You always do. And when you do, we'll be waiting."

Caelan didn't stop. He didn't turn back. He couldn't afford to. Not now, not when everything he had come to believe was at stake.

He made his way quickly to the stables, his heart pounding in his chest as he approached the horse he had prepared for the journey ahead. Lyra would be waiting for him. They had decided to move forward, to face the future together. They had no time to waste, no time to question their choices. The world was shifting beneath their feet, and the kingdoms were on the brink of war. They had to act now, or everything would fall apart.

He saddled the horse with quick, practiced movements, his mind still reeling from his conversation with Orin. The fire of the kingdom, of Emberfall, was still burning within him, but it no longer felt like home. The weight of duty was a heavy chain, and as much as he had once worn it proudly, it now felt like a shackle, holding him back from something greater.

Lyra. The prophecy. The future they would carve together.

His resolve hardened, and for the first time, he felt a sense of clarity that cut through the fog of doubt. He had made his choice. There was no going back.

He mounted the horse and rode through the gates of

Emberfall without looking back.

As the castle disappeared behind him, the weight of his past began to feel lighter. The path ahead was uncertain, but it was his to walk. And with Lyra by his side, he would face whatever came next—no matter the cost.

The winds of war were gathering, but so too was the storm within him, and he was ready to embrace it.

# Nine

# The Waters Rise

The moon hung high above the water, a pale, distant witness to the storm that churned inside of Lyra. She stood at the edge of the sacred waters of Tidewell, her heart pounding in her chest. The waves rippled gently at her feet, their pull constant, as if they had a voice of their own, whispering secrets she could not yet understand. The ancient waters—where the power of her ancestors had once thrived—now seemed as restless as the magic surging within her.

Lyra had always known that her connection to the water was more than just power—it was a legacy, a bloodline that ran deep, tied to the very core of the kingdom of Tidewell. But as her powers had grown stronger, so too had the fear that she was losing control of them. The water, once a soothing, familiar presence, now felt like a tempest inside her, dangerous and unpredictable. It had taken everything to keep it contained, and even now, she could feel it—beneath her skin, pulling at her, testing her resolve.

She inhaled deeply, feeling the cool night air fill her lungs, but it did little to calm her racing heart. The path she had chosen to take—to come here, to the sacred waters—was not one she had taken lightly. These waters held secrets. Old magic. And if there was any hope for her to master the magic within her, she needed to confront them, to learn their truth, no matter how painful.

The wind stirred, and the waves grew restless. Lyra took a step forward, her boots sinking into the soft earth of the riverbank, her senses heightened. Her mind was heavy with the weight of the decision she had made. Caelan had wanted to come with her. He had pleaded with her to wait, to not go alone. But this journey was hers. She needed to understand her powers, to learn what was at stake for them both.

As she stepped further into the water, she could feel the power of the sacred place enveloping her, the ancient magic that lay beneath the surface calling to her. It was as if the waters themselves were aware of her presence, waiting for her to take the next step, to reach for the truth that had been hidden for centuries.

"Show me," she whispered, her voice barely audible over the rising wind. "Show me what I need to know."

The water at her feet began to stir, the waves growing stronger, swirling around her ankles, and then— suddenly—there was silence. The air grew heavy, the world around her still. In that moment, she felt something shift deep inside her, as if the very fabric of the world had opened up. The water before her rippled, and the surface shimmered like glass, reflecting the moonlight in strange, fractured patterns.

And then, the vision came.

A flash of images—of fire and water, clashing in a violent storm. She saw the kingdoms of Emberfall and Tidewell, the two forces locked in a struggle that threatened to consume everything in its wake. But amidst the chaos, she saw herself and Caelan, standing together, their hands entwined, their powers swirling around them—fire and water, locked in an eternal dance. The prophecy. The sacrifice. It was all there, laid bare before her eyes.

The vision blurred and shifted. A figure appeared, cloaked in shadows. His face was obscured, but his presence was overwhelming, his power palpable. The figure raised his hand, and the water around her began to rise, swirling into a vortex. Lyra's heart raced, her breath shallow. The figure's voice echoed in her mind, like a distant whisper.

"To unite fire and water," the voice intoned, "one must die. It is the cost of the prophecy. The balance cannot be achieved without sacrifice."

The words struck her like a physical blow. The water surged higher, crashing against her, pulling her deeper into the vision. "No," she gasped, shaking her head, but the voice continued, relentless, unyielding.

"The prophecy binds you, Lyra. Your power, your connection to the water, it is the key. But it is also your curse. The fire must be tempered by the water, and the water must be tempered by the fire. Only then will the kingdoms be united, and the war will end. But one of you must die."

Lyra's heart stopped. The words reverberated in her mind, over and over, until they felt like they were carved into her soul. *One of you must die.* The choice was clear. And the weight of it crashed down on her like a wave, threatening to drown her in its enormity.

She stumbled backward, her breath coming in ragged gasps, as the vision began to fade. The waters around her grew still again, and the wind died down, leaving only the sound of her own heartbeat in her ears. But the words—the terrible, painful truth—remained.

The prophecy was a trap. A cruel trick, hidden beneath layers of power and magic. And the cost of uniting fire and water was a sacrifice neither she nor Caelan had ever anticipated.

Lyra stood in the water, the cold biting at her skin, her hands trembling. The weight of what she had learned was suffocating, a crushing force that threatened to undo everything. She felt the waters around her, their pulse—wild and untamed—and for the first time, she wasn't sure if she could control it. She wasn't sure if she could control herself.

A cold tear slid down her cheek as the reality of the vision sank in. She had known the prophecy would not be simple, but she had never imagined that it would demand such a terrible price.

She couldn't lose him. She couldn't lose Caelan.

But if they were to unite their powers, if they were to bring peace to the kingdoms, then one of them had to die. And the decision—*the choice*—wasn't hers alone. It was theirs. And it would tear them apart.

"Lyra."

The sound of her name broke through the fog of her thoughts. She turned, startled, to see a shadowy figure standing at the edge of the sacred waters. It was Caelan. His figure was framed by the moonlight, his face unreadable, though the concern in his eyes was clear.

"What are you doing here?" Lyra asked, her voice strained, the pain in her chest almost unbearable.

"I felt it," he said, his voice low. "I felt the storm rising. I had to come."

He stepped toward her, the warmth of his presence cutting through the coldness of the water. But Lyra stepped back, her heart hammering in her chest. She couldn't bear to look at him, not when the truth was still so fresh in her mind. Not when she had just learned that their love, their union, could be the very thing that destroyed them.

"You shouldn't have come, Caelan," she said, her voice trembling. "You can't be here. This place—it's dangerous."

He looked at her, confusion flickering in his eyes. "What do you mean? I don't understand."

She swallowed hard, trying to steady her breath. The truth was too much to bear alone, but she wasn't sure she could say it out loud. "The prophecy," she began, her voice soft but filled with an undeniable weight. "It's not just a union. It's a sacrifice. One of us has to die to make it work. To bring balance between fire and water, one of us must die."

Caelan's eyes darkened, his jaw tightening as he stepped closer, the heat from his body pushing against the coldness of the water. "No," he said, his voice low but filled with fury. "That's not possible. We—"

But Lyra shook her head, her breath catching in her throat. "It's true, Caelan. I saw it. I felt it. This prophecy, this magic— it isn't just about us. It's about something much bigger. And one of us will have to pay the price."

For a moment, there was silence, the weight of her words hanging between them like a physical force. Caelan reached for her, his hand trembling as it hovered near hers, but she pulled away, her heart aching as she saw the pain in his eyes.

"Don't you see?" she whispered. "We've been caught in something we can't control. The prophecy—it's a trap. And if we're not careful, it will destroy us."

Caelan's eyes burned with something fierce—something that matched the fire inside him. "I won't let it destroy us. I won't let anything tear us apart, Lyra. Not even the prophecy."

But his words, though filled with love and desperation, did nothing to quell the storm inside her. She could feel the waters rise again, threatening to pull her under. She could feel the weight of the decision that loomed ahead, and it felt like an anchor, dragging her down deeper and deeper.

She stepped back, her eyes brimming with unshed tears. "I don't know if I can do this, Caelan," she whispered. "I don't know if I can live with the cost."

He reached for her again, his hands trembling, and this time, she didn't pull away. His touch was warm, grounding her in the chaos, in the uncertainty that had taken root in her heart.

"We'll figure it out," he said softly, his voice filled with determination. "Together."

But even as his words echoed in her mind, Lyra knew that the path ahead was uncertain. The storm had only just begun, and it was already pulling them in different directions. She didn't know if they could survive the truth of the prophecy. She didn't know if they could come out of this whole.

But as Caelan held her close, the warmth of his presence somehow calming the storm inside her, she allowed herself to believe, if only for a moment, that they could survive this. That together, they could face whatever came next.

And yet, deep inside, she couldn't shake the feeling that the greatest battle was still ahead of them.

Lyra stood still in Caelan's embrace, the warmth of his touch grounding her, even as the storm inside her raged, threatening to drown her in uncertainty. His arms around her were strong, a lifeline amidst the chaos, but they couldn't protect her from the weight of the prophecy—the sacrifice it demanded.

"I can't lose you, Lyra," Caelan whispered, his voice rough, as if the words themselves were a confession of something deeper, something he had never fully said before.

She closed her eyes, the familiar scent of smoke and salt mingling in the air, but she didn't find comfort in it this time. The weight of the world felt heavier with every passing breath, each one more labored than the last. She had known that there would be a cost, but the reality of it—the harsh truth of the sacrifice that stood between them—felt like an anchor pulling her under.

"I don't want to lose you either," she murmured, her voice barely audible against the howling wind. "But we may not have a choice."

Caelan pulled back slightly, his hands still resting on her shoulders, his gaze searching hers. The fire within him was unmistakable, his determination to fight for their love burning bright. But in his eyes, there was something else—a flicker of the same fear that had been slowly creeping into her heart.

"You don't have to face this alone," he said, his voice fierce but gentle. "Whatever it is, we'll figure it out. Together."

The word *together* felt like a promise, a fragile lifeline that she wanted to hold onto. But as much as she wished to believe in it, the reality of the prophecy, the truth she had seen in the sacred waters, weighed heavily on her. She could already feel the consequences of their love—of their connection. The storm had been an outward manifestation of what was building inside them. Their combined powers had already begun to tear at the seams of the world. And if they were to unite fire and water, it would only be through a terrible price.

"I don't know if we *can* figure it out," she whispered, her voice breaking as she took a step back, away from him. The sudden distance felt unbearable, but it was the only way she could think clearly. "Caelan, the prophecy—it's not just about us. It's about the kingdoms. If we fail… if we can't find a way to make the prophecy work… the war will swallow everything. But if we do succeed… then one of us has to die."

The words were heavy, sinking into the space between them like a lead weight. Caelan's face paled, his breath catching as the full weight of what she was saying hit him.

"No," he said, shaking his head, his hands trembling at his sides. "There has to be another way. There's always another way."

Lyra's chest tightened as she watched him, her heart aching with the depth of the love she felt for him. She wanted to believe him, wanted to believe that there could be some escape from the darkness that the prophecy had cast upon them. But she couldn't. Not now.

"I wish I could believe that," she said softly, her voice barely above a whisper. "But the waters showed me the truth, Caelan. And the truth is… one of us will have to die. To bring the kingdoms together. To stop the war. We can't change that."

The silence between them was deafening, as if the entire world had paused, waiting for their next move. The wind picked up again, and the waters at her feet began to churn once more, as though echoing the chaos within her.

"Lyra," Caelan began, his voice raw, trembling with emotion, "don't… please don't say that. We'll find another way. We'll—"

He was cut off by the sharp sound of footsteps behind them. Lyra's heart lurched as she turned, instinctively stepping back from Caelan, as though the physical distance could somehow shield them from the truth.

Thorne emerged from the shadows, his expression unreadable, his face etched with worry. The ever-present tension in his eyes spoke volumes. Behind him, Aric stood, his arms crossed, a silent observer to the exchange between Caelan and Lyra.

"Sorry to interrupt," Thorne said, his voice tight with urgency, "but we don't have much time. Ivor's forces have been spotted just outside the capital. They're getting ready to march, and we need to make a move now."

Lyra's stomach tightened at the mention of Ivor's name. The reality of their situation hit her with a jolt—there was no time for indecision, no time for hesitation. She had to make a choice, and she had to make it now. For Emberfall, for the prophecy, for Caelan.

"We can't afford to waste any more time," Thorne continued, his voice sharp, his gaze flicking between the two of them. "We've fought too long for this. Too many people are counting on us to stop this war."

Lyra nodded numbly, the words sinking in, though her mind was still miles away. She could hear Caelan's voice, soft and insistent, trying to reach her.

"Lyra," he said, his voice low and filled with quiet desperation. "Please. Let's just… talk about this. There has to be another way."

But she couldn't—she couldn't bear to look at him now, not when the truth had settled so deeply in her heart. She wanted to believe in them, in their love. But the reality of the prophecy loomed over them both like an inevitable storm.

She turned to Thorne, her voice steady despite the fear swirling inside her. "I'm ready. I'll do whatever it takes."

Thorne's expression softened slightly, but he didn't hesitate. "Good," he said, his voice firm, but with a hint of warmth. "Let's go. We've got a battle to win."

As they made their way out of the sacred waters, Lyra could feel the storm within her still raging. But this time, it wasn't just the elements she had to contend with. It was the weight of the prophecy, the knowledge that what they were about to do could change everything.

And yet, even as the fear gnawed at her, she couldn't deny the truth that had taken root in her heart: no matter what happened, no matter how dark the path became, she couldn't turn her back on Caelan. Not now. Not ever.

They reached the edge of the sacred grounds, the wind whipping around them as the rest of the rebels gathered their things and prepared to move out. Lyra stood beside Caelan, her hand instinctively seeking his, though it felt like a fragile thread between them.

"Whatever happens," she said quietly, her voice trembling, "we face this together."

Caelan squeezed her hand, his touch warm and grounding. But even as their fingers intertwined, a part of her knew— knew deep down—that the cost of the prophecy would be far greater than either of them could fully understand.

The air grew heavier as they moved toward the waiting horses. The kingdom of Emberfall was on the brink of war, and the prophecy's grip on them both tightened with each passing moment. The storm, once just a shadow on the horizon, was now crashing toward them with the force of the sea itself.

And Lyra knew that no matter how strong their love was, no matter how fiercely they fought to stay together, the world around them was about to change forever.

The waters had risen. The prophecy had begun to take its toll. And there was no turning back.

**Ten**

# The Flames of Sacrifice

The air in the cave was thick with heat, heavy with the weight of ancient power. The crackling of fire and the distant echoes of water rushing somewhere below reverberated through the stone walls. Lyra stood at the heart of the cave, her breath shallow, every nerve in her body alive with tension. The prophecy had brought them here, to this moment, this terrible moment that neither she nor Caelan could escape.

Behind her, the torches flickered on the walls, casting long shadows across the cold stone. She could feel Caelan's presence before he even spoke, the warmth of his fire just behind her, like a living, breathing thing. The flames that always seemed to cling to him had grown more intense, as if they could sense the danger, the impending clash between them both. The fire and water, their powers so closely intertwined, were now at a breaking point. But neither of them could escape the truth of the prophecy—they were bound by fate, bound by love, and now bound by the cost of it all.

Caelan stepped forward, his eyes dark and filled with a quiet intensity that made her chest tighten. His face was hard, his features set in a mask of determination, but she could see the storm brewing within him—the same storm that had been swirling in her own heart since the vision, since the revelation that one of them would have to die.

"We can't keep doing this, Lyra," he said, his voice hoarse, as though the very words were a struggle. "I can't keep pretending like there's another way. We've known for days, since we learned the truth. The prophecy is clear. It's either you or me."

Lyra turned toward him, her eyes locked on his, and in that moment, she saw the raw fear behind his gaze—the fear of losing everything. She could feel it too, in the depths of her bones, a fear that gnawed at her every waking moment. She had known this truth from the moment she saw the vision in the sacred waters of Tidewell. The prophecy was not just about bringing fire and water together—it was about sacrifice. The cost of unity was death. One of them would have to die to bring peace to the kingdoms.

"I won't let you do it, Caelan," she said, her voice trembling but firm. "I won't let you be the one to die. Not for me. Not for anyone."

Caelan took a step closer, his presence overwhelming, the heat of his body nearly suffocating. "And I won't let you die, Lyra," he replied, his voice low and filled with a quiet rage. "You think I'll stand by and let you sacrifice yourself? You think I'll let you go through with this for the sake of some prophecy?"

They stood there, the space between them thick with unsaid

words, with the weight of the world hanging in the balance. Lyra's heart raced in her chest, each beat echoing the storm within her. The fire and water, the forces they wielded, had never felt more dangerous, more unpredictable, than they did now. It wasn't just their powers—it was their love. Their connection. It was what tied them together, but it was also what threatened to tear them apart.

"I love you," Caelan whispered, his voice raw, vulnerable. The words hung between them, like an offering, a plea for her to understand. "And I'll do anything to protect you. If it means giving my life to stop this war, to save you and the kingdom, then I'll do it. Don't you see? I can't lose you. You're everything to me."

Lyra felt a cold shiver run through her at the intensity of his words. The declaration of love was both a gift and a curse, an expression of the bond they shared but also the enormity of the decision they faced. She could feel the tears stinging at the back of her eyes, but she refused to let them fall. This wasn't about emotion. This was about life and death.

"Caelan," she breathed, taking a step toward him, her hand reaching for his. "You *are* everything to me. But I can't let you sacrifice yourself. We promised each other we wouldn't run from this, from the truth. But you can't make that choice alone. I won't let you."

Her fingers trembled as they touched his, the heat of his fire burning through her skin. The touch, the connection, was both comforting and agonizing. It was like a living thing, this love, this magic that had grown between them. She felt his heart racing beneath her hand, the same uncertainty, the same love reflected in his gaze.

"Then what do we do?" Caelan's voice cracked, his eyes

searching hers, desperate for an answer, for a way out that they both knew didn't exist. "What do we do, Lyra? How do we stop this prophecy from destroying us?"

Lyra swallowed hard, her heart breaking as the weight of their choices pressed down on her chest. The reality of the prophecy—the truth of it—was something neither of them could deny anymore. She had seen the vision. She had felt the call of the water, the ancient magic that demanded balance, that demanded sacrifice. And no matter how much they fought against it, it would still come. One of them would have to die.

"I don't know," she said, her voice barely above a whisper, the words slipping from her lips like the last remnants of hope. "I don't know how to stop it, Caelan. I don't know how to fix this."

The silence stretched between them, heavy and thick, as the fire and water seemed to hum with a shared understanding. The cost of their love, the cost of the prophecy, was too great. Too painful.

But then, as if driven by something both primal and necessary, Caelan reached for her, pulling her close, his hands framing her face. She gasped at the intensity of his touch, the fire that burned just beneath his skin radiating through her, but it was the depth of his gaze that held her. It was as if he was trying to memorize her, trying to imprint every detail of her onto his soul, so that even in death, he would carry her with him.

"Please," Caelan whispered, his voice thick with emotion. "If we have to make this choice, if one of us has to die, then let it be me. Please."

Lyra's heart shattered at the words, the depth of his sacrifice, the love that burned so fiercely inside him. She reached up, pressing her hands to his chest, feeling the frantic beat of his heart beneath her palms.

"No," she whispered fiercely, her tears finally spilling over, her voice breaking. "I can't let you, Caelan. I can't lose you."

The pain that radiated from her words seemed to cut through the air like a blade. The moment stretched, an eternity of love, fear, and heartache, and in that moment, Lyra knew that the decision they were facing was not just about the kingdoms, not just about fire and water. It was about them. About what they were willing to sacrifice for each other.

Before she could say anything more, Caelan leaned down, his lips brushing against hers in a kiss that was both desperate and tender, a final plea, a declaration of the love that had defined them. The kiss deepened, a moment of passion and emotion that shook them both to their core. Lyra felt everything in that kiss—the love, the sacrifice, the deep, unspoken fear of what lay ahead.

But it was also a promise.

A promise that no matter what happened, they would face it together.

When the kiss finally broke, both of them gasping for air, Lyra looked into Caelan's eyes, her heart full of love and sorrow. She knew that the road ahead would be filled with more pain, more loss, but she also knew that they had come this far because of the bond they shared. No matter what happened, they would face it together.

"I won't let you die," Lyra whispered, her voice trembling but filled with conviction. "Not like this. We'll find another way. We'll fight the prophecy, Caelan. We'll fight it together."

Caelan's gaze softened, but there was a sadness in his eyes that mirrored her own. He gently cupped her face, his thumb brushing away the tear that had fallen. "I'll do anything for you, Lyra. I'll fight for you until my last breath. But if it comes to it… if I have to… I'll make the sacrifice. For you. For us. For the future."

Lyra shook her head, her tears falling freely now. "No," she said, her voice shaking with emotion. "I can't live with that. I can't lose you. I won't."

The tension in the air was unbearable. It was as if the world itself was holding its breath, waiting for them to make the impossible choice. But there was no choice. Not one that they could bear.

"I love you," Lyra whispered, the words slipping from her lips as she pressed herself closer to him, feeling his warmth, his fire. "I love you more than anything in this world. And I can't lose you."

Caelan's arms tightened around her, pulling her closer still, his fire meeting her water in a delicate dance of warmth and coolness, fire and ice. Their powers, their bond, seemed to pulse between them, an energy that was both terrifying and beautiful.

And in that moment, as they stood there, locked in each other's arms, the truth settled between them like an unspoken promise: the battle ahead would not just be against their enemies. It would be a battle against fate itself.

But no matter what the cost, no matter what the prophecy demanded, they would face it together. For their love, for their kingdoms, and for the future they had fought so hard to build.

Even if it meant sacrificing everything they had.

And in that heart-wrenching moment, as their world seemed to spin toward destruction, Lyra knew one thing for certain: whatever the future held, their love would be the flame that burned through the darkness.

No matter the cost.

The air around them seemed to crackle with an energy that wasn't entirely their own.  Caelan held her tightly, as if by sheer force of will, he could keep both of them tethered to the moment, to each other. Lyra could feel the warmth of his fire seeping into her skin, but it didn't burn her. Instead, it was comforting, like a promise. And yet, deep in her heart, she could feel the cold pull of the truth—the prophecy, the inevitable choice.

Their kiss had burned with desperation, but also a kind of finality, a plea for a future they weren't sure they could have. The love between them had always felt like something that could conquer anything, but this—this was different. This was a test of everything they had built. She could see it in his eyes. He wasn't just fighting for their love anymore. He was preparing to fight against destiny itself.

For a long moment, neither of them spoke. The only sound was the distant roar of water rushing beneath the cave, the steady beat of their hearts, and the soft crackle of fire. Caelan pulled back slightly, but only enough to see her face, his hand still cupping her cheek, his thumb brushing away another tear.

"Lyra," he said, his voice hoarse, strained with emotion, "you have to understand. If the choice comes—if it's truly between us, I'll—" His voice faltered, the words seemingly choking him. He couldn't finish the sentence, couldn't bring himself to say what had to be said. The truth was too painful, too raw.

She swallowed, her chest tightening with a mixture of love and fear. "Caelan," she whispered, her voice barely audible, "I can't—don't say it. We don't know what will happen. There has to be another way. We're not bound to this prophecy. We *can* fight it."

He shook his head, a look of pain and resignation flashing across his face. "I wish I could believe that, Lyra. I really do. But the waters… they showed me too much. The truth is clear. We are the key to ending this war, but at a cost. I don't care what it is. I just… I don't want to lose you."

His words hit her like a hammer, each syllable driving deep into her heart. She wanted to fight back, to scream that they *could* find another way, that this wasn't the end, that they were meant to be together. But she couldn't lie to him. Not anymore. The vision had been clear. The prophecy was not a simple fate—it was a sacrifice, one that neither of them could escape.

She stepped back from him, her breath shaky as she tried to steady herself. Her body trembled, but it wasn't from the cold. It was from the sheer weight of the decision that hung between them.

"Please," she begged, her voice breaking. "Don't make that decision for both of us. I won't let you die, Caelan. I won't."

His fiery gaze softened, the heat in his eyes dimming slightly as his hands fell to his sides. But there was something else there, something deeper—a look of helplessness. "Lyra, you're asking me to let you die. And I can't do that. I can't live with that choice."

Her chest tightened at the thought, the unbearable weight of it making it hard to breathe. "But I can't lose you," she said, her voice barely a whisper. "I've already lost so much—so much of myself—just by being part of this. I can't lose you, too."

Caelan's jaw tightened, and he reached for her again, pulling her into his embrace once more, his arms around her tight, almost desperate. She clung to him, feeling the rhythm of his heart beat against her chest, the steady thrum of life, of love, of everything they had fought for.

"I love you," he murmured, the words barely a breath, but it was enough to make her heart shatter. "And I'll do anything for you."

"I love you too," she whispered back, pressing her face against his chest, feeling the heat of his fire through the fabric of his shirt. But even as the words left her mouth, she knew the truth. The prophecy was still there, hanging over them like a dark shadow, and no matter how much they loved each other, no matter how much they *wanted* to be together, they couldn't escape the cost.

She closed her eyes, the tears coming now, rolling down her cheeks in hot, uncontrollable streams. She felt his fingers gently brush through her hair, soothing her, but it wasn't enough to quiet the storm inside. The fire and the water—both raging inside them—had never felt more dangerous, more volatile. Every touch, every kiss, only served to remind her that they were both burning alive.

"I can't lose you," she repeated, her voice breaking. "Please. I won't be able to survive it. Please."

Caelan held her tighter, and for a long time, neither of them spoke. The silence between them was filled with unspoken fears, unacknowledged truths. It was the silence of lovers who had reached the breaking point, who knew that no matter how desperately they clung to each other, fate had already cast its shadow over them.

Finally, Caelan pulled back slightly, his eyes searching hers, the flicker of fire still burning in his gaze. "What if..." he began, his voice hesitant. "What if we don't have to sacrifice? What if there's another way? We've beaten the odds before. Maybe we can do it again. Together."

Lyra searched his eyes, her heart breaking all over again. "We can't fight fate forever, Caelan," she said softly, her voice raw with emotion. "The prophecy is bigger than us. It's bigger than our love. The kingdoms, the fire and the water—they've been at odds for centuries. And it's only through us that they can be united. But one of us…" Her voice caught in her throat, the words hard to say, even harder to hear. "One of us has to die."

Caelan shook his head, his expression pained, as though the very idea of losing her was something he couldn't even bear to comprehend. "I won't let it be you. I won't."

She felt her chest tighten, her breath caught in her throat as the rawness of their emotions crashed over her. "Then we'll both die," she whispered, her voice trembling. "If one of us dies, then we both will. Because I won't live without you, Caelan. I won't."

The words hung between them, and for a long moment, Caelan didn't speak. The pain in his eyes was a mirror to the pain in her own heart. They were trapped in a world that demanded sacrifice, a world where their love wasn't enough to change the course of fate.

Finally, Caelan took a deep breath, as if steeling himself for something. He cupped her face in his hands, his gaze never leaving hers. "We can't change the prophecy. But maybe we can change what it means. Maybe we can find a way to make it right. Together."

Lyra closed her eyes, pressing her forehead to his. "I don't know if we can," she whispered. "But I won't give up. I won't stop fighting for us. For our love."

And in that moment, with the flames of their love raging

around them and the waters rising between them, they both understood the truth. The future was uncertain, and the price of their love was still yet to be paid.  But whatever it was, whatever choice they would have to make, they would face it together.

Caelan kissed her then, a kiss that was not desperate or final, but one filled with all the love and sorrow and hope they could no longer hide. It was a kiss of surrender, of acceptance. Of understanding.

And in the silence that followed, the world seemed to pause, holding its breath, waiting for the next step to be taken.

Their love was all they had left.

And in the end, it would be their love that would determine if they survived the flames of sacrifice.

# Eleven

# A Path of Shadows

The air in the underground passageway was heavy, damp, and cold, the stone walls slick with the remnants of water seeping through cracks in the earth. Lyra felt the chill in her bones, but it wasn't the cold of the cave that made her shiver. It was the heavy weight of the darkness around them, the suffocating silence that pressed in on all sides. The tension was so thick she could almost taste it, like the promise of something terrible lingering just beyond reach.

They had been running for days, since the attack on their camp by Ivor's forces. The war had escalated quickly—faster than anyone had anticipated—and now they were forced to flee deeper into the heart of the kingdom, away from prying eyes and the ever-growing danger that loomed behind them. The rebellion's army was fractured, scattered in every direction, and they could trust no one—not even their closest allies. Not anymore.

Caelan walked beside her, his presence a constant, grounding force in the midst of the chaos. But even his warmth, his fire, couldn't completely dispel the unease that gnawed at Lyra's gut. She could feel the tension in his shoulders, the way his hand never strayed far from the hilt of his sword. He was as aware as she was that their enemies were closing in, that every step they took brought them closer to an inevitable confrontation.

"We need to keep moving," Caelan said, his voice low, barely above a whisper. His eyes flickered to the narrow passage ahead, his mind clearly already calculating their next move. "Ivor's forces are close. We won't have much time."

Lyra nodded, but her mind was far from the present. The truth of the prophecy, the knowledge that one of them must die to bring balance, weighed heavily on her thoughts. She had spent every moment since their last conversation with Caelan trying to understand the prophecy, to find a way to make sense of the sacrifice it demanded. But no matter how hard she tried, the truth remained elusive, hidden in the shadows, just out of reach.

The air grew colder as they ventured deeper into the underground ruins, the ancient stone around them old and worn, covered in moss and creeping vines. The walls seemed to close in as they descended, the space growing smaller and darker with each step.

"Do you think we'll be safe here?" Lyra asked, her voice almost a whisper, as if the darkness itself might overhear her. She kept her eyes on the ground, scanning for any movement, anything out of the ordinary. She could feel the pull of the water, but even the comforting rush of her own magic didn't ease the tightness in her chest.

Caelan's jaw tightened, his eyes scanning the shadows. "For now, yes. But not for long. We'll need to find a way out before Ivor's scouts reach this area. They won't stop until they find us."

They reached a small alcove in the passageway, a natural stone shelf that provided some shelter from the elements. Lyra sank down onto the cold stone floor, her back against the wall, her hands trembling slightly as she tried to gather her thoughts. Caelan stood at the entrance of the alcove, his body tense, his eyes darting from shadow to shadow, ever watchful.

"We need to be prepared for the worst," he said, his voice tight. "Ivor will stop at nothing. And if he learns the truth about the prophecy—about what it demands—he will do whatever it takes to stop us."

Lyra nodded again, but the fear in her heart refused to fade. The prophecy was a weapon, something Ivor would use to his advantage. And they were running out of time.

A sudden sound broke the silence—a faint scraping of metal against stone. Lyra froze, her heart pounding in her chest. Caelan immediately tensed, his body going still as he raised a hand to silence her. His eyes met hers, and in that brief moment, they shared a silent understanding. They weren't alone.

The sound grew louder, closer. Footsteps—too soft, too careful to be their allies. Lyra's breath caught in her throat. Was it Ivor's men? Had they found them already?

She reached instinctively for the water, feeling it pulse beneath her skin, ready to protect herself, ready to strike if necessary. Caelan stepped forward, his hand drawing his blade from its sheath, the steel gleaming faintly in the dim light.

"Stay behind me," he whispered, his voice low and commanding.

Lyra moved behind him, her magic swirling around her, her fingers tingling with the familiar, dangerous power of the water. They waited, the seconds stretching out like hours, until the shadows finally revealed their source.

A figure emerged from the darkness, moving slowly, cautiously. Lyra's heart skipped a beat, her body instinctively bracing for a fight. But then, the figure stepped fully into the light, and Lyra's breath caught in her throat.

It was Thorne. His face was pale, his clothes torn and stained with dirt, but it was unmistakably him.

"Thorne?" Caelan's voice was filled with a mixture of disbelief and relief. "What the hell are you doing here? You're supposed to be with the others."

Thorne's gaze flickered between Caelan and Lyra, his expression unreadable. He stepped fully into the alcove, his footsteps slow, deliberate. He didn't seem surprised to see them, but there was something in his eyes—something cold, something calculating—that made Lyra's heart sink.

"I came to find you," Thorne said, his voice flat, almost lifeless. "You're both in more danger than you know."

Lyra frowned, her mind racing. "What do you mean? We're running from Ivor's forces. We don't have time to—"

Thorne cut her off, his eyes narrowing. "It's not Ivor you should be worried about. It's the prophecy. The truth of it. The hidden betrayal."

Lyra's blood ran cold. She felt Caelan tense beside her, his body stiffening with the sudden tension in the air. "What are you talking about?" Caelan asked, his voice low, edged with suspicion.

Thorne's gaze flickered away for a moment, as though

weighing his next words carefully. "I've been investigating the prophecy. The real one. The one no one talks about. The one that was sealed away long ago. The one that's been kept hidden from both kingdoms."

Lyra's pulse quickened. "What do you know about it?"

Thorne hesitated, his gaze flickering toward the entrance of the alcove, as though afraid of being overheard. "I know enough to understand that the prophecy wasn't meant to unite fire and water. It was meant to destroy them. To ensure that neither kingdom could ever truly claim the power of both elements."

Caelan's grip on his sword tightened. "What are you saying?"

Thorne stepped closer, lowering his voice. "I'm saying that the prophecy isn't about saving the kingdoms. It's about ensuring that one of them—the one with the true power—dies. And I've just discovered who that is."

The words hung between them like a heavy weight, suffocating the air in the small alcove. Lyra's heart skipped a beat, her mind racing. "Who?"

Thorne's gaze met hers, and in that moment, she saw it—the cold, calculated look of someone who had made up his mind, who had already chosen his side.

"It's you, Lyra," he said, his voice cold and filled with a quiet finality. "You're the one who has to die."

The world seemed to shatter around her. Lyra's breath caught in her throat, her entire body going numb. She stumbled backward, the weight of his words crashing into her like a tidal wave.

"No," Caelan growled, his voice thick with disbelief. "You're lying. This is a trick. You've always been with us."

Thorne's eyes flickered with something that might have been

guilt, but it was quickly masked by the coldness that had taken over his demeanor. "I never wanted this, Caelan. But I've seen the truth. The betrayal goes deeper than we thought. One of you has to die. And it's not going to be me."

Lyra couldn't breathe. She couldn't think. The world was spinning around her, every word Thorne spoke sinking into her like a blade. She turned to Caelan, her hand reaching for his, her heart hammering in her chest.

"No," she whispered, her voice trembling. "Caelan, please. We can't… we can't let this happen."

Caelan's face was a mask of fury, his grip on his sword tightening as he stepped forward. "You've been working with them, haven't you, Thorne?" His voice was low, a deadly calm that sent chills through the air. "You've been playing both sides."

Thorne's expression flickered for just a moment, the mask of indifference cracking. "I did what I had to do. We've all been pawns in this game, Caelan. But now we're out of time. The prophecy is coming for us, and one of you is going to die to make sure it's fulfilled."

Lyra's heart broke. She couldn't breathe, couldn't think. The world had tilted on its axis, and she was losing her grip. She looked at Caelan, seeing the same devastation mirrored in his eyes.

"Caelan, please," she whispered, stepping toward him, her voice barely audible. "Don't listen to him. We're not enemies. We're not."

Caelan took a step back, his hand dropping to his side as the weight of what Thorne had said crashed down on him. "We have to decide, Lyra. Now. Before it's too late."

The weight of the betrayal hung over them all, suffocating

and cold. They had never felt more alone, more vulnerable, than they did in this moment. The future was uncertain, and everything they had fought for—everything they had hoped for—now seemed like a distant, unreachable dream.

And as the shadows closed in around them, Lyra knew one thing for sure: the path ahead would be the hardest test of their love yet. And the cost of it might be more than they were willing to pay.

The cold air of the underground cavern seemed to press in on them, thick and suffocating. The dim light from the torches flickered, casting shadows that danced across the ancient stone walls, reflecting the chaos in their minds. Lyra stood motionless, her hand still reaching out toward Caelan, but the weight of Thorne's words had lodged themselves deep within her chest, a heavy, unshakable truth that threatened to tear them all apart.

Caelan's face was a mask of barely controlled fury. His eyes, usually so filled with fire and determination, were now clouded with doubt and betrayal. His gaze flickered from Thorne to Lyra, the tension between them palpable, the unsaid words hanging in the air like a noose tightening around them.

"You're telling me," Caelan said, his voice low, dangerous, "that we've been running, fighting, bleeding for this war... for a prophecy that demands Lyra's death?"

Thorne met his gaze, unflinching, but there was a flicker of something in his eyes—regret, maybe, or sorrow—but it was gone in an instant. "That's exactly what I'm saying," Thorne replied coldly. "The prophecy isn't about saving anyone. It's about ensuring balance, and that balance comes at a cost. Lyra was always the one destined to die to bring that balance. And if we don't make that sacrifice, the war will never end. The kingdoms will burn, and everything we've fought for will be meaningless."

Lyra felt the world tilt beneath her feet, her breath coming in shallow gasps. The pain in her chest seemed to spread outward, suffocating her from the inside. How had it come to this? How had they gone from fighting for their love, their future, to facing the very real possibility that one of them would have to die to save the world?

"I won't let it happen," she said, her voice trembling but fierce. She turned to Caelan, her eyes desperate for him to understand, for him to see beyond the pain of Thorne's words. "I won't let you give up your life for me. I won't."

Caelan's hand clenched into a fist at his side, his jaw tight with frustration. "And I won't let you sacrifice yourself, Lyra," he said, his voice hoarse with emotion. "We've been through too much, fought too hard, to let this prophecy tear us apart. There has to be another way. There has to be."

But even as he spoke, Lyra could see the doubt in his eyes. She could see the way the weight of Thorne's words had begun to sink in, the possibility that they were running out of options. The war was on the brink of consuming everything they had, and the price of peace—of victory—was more than they were ready to pay.

Thorne stepped closer, his eyes cold and unfeeling. "You're wasting time," he said. "The more you resist, the worse it will get. Ivor's forces are already closing in on this position. If you don't accept the truth of the prophecy, you'll be fighting not just against the kingdoms but against the very forces that created this world. And you'll lose. All of you."

Caelan's hand tightened around his sword hilt. "You think

we're going to just give up? Let it all burn?" His voice was sharp, the heat of his fire simmering just beneath the surface. "You're wrong, Thorne. You're wrong about everything."

Thorne's expression didn't change, but Lyra could see the slight twitch in his jaw, the flicker of emotion in his eyes that betrayed his cold exterior. "I'm not the enemy here, Caelan. I'm telling you what has to be done. This isn't about loyalty. It's about survival. If you want to see the world saved, if you want to stop the endless war, then one of you—Lyra, or you—must die. That's the only way it ends."

Lyra's chest tightened. She reached out, placing her hand on Caelan's arm, willing him to see reason, to understand. "Please, Caelan. We've been through too much. We can't let this prophecy define us. There has to be a way out."

But even as she spoke, she felt the weight of Thorne's words creeping into her heart, taking root in the darkest corners of her mind. She knew—deep down—that there was no escaping the truth. The prophecy had been set in motion long before they had ever met, and they had been caught in its grip from the very first moment their paths had crossed.

Caelan turned to face her, his eyes filled with an intensity that made her heart skip a beat. "We won't let it tear us apart," he said, his voice fierce. "We'll find another way. We'll—"

A sudden crash interrupted him, the sound of distant footsteps and shouting echoing down the narrow tunnels of the ruins. Lyra's heart skipped a beat. They were running out of time.

"Ivor's forces are here," Thorne said quietly, his face grim. "We need to go. Now."

Lyra turned to Caelan, her breath coming faster, panic rising in her chest. They couldn't stay here. Not with the forces closing in. Not when their enemies were so close.

"Come on," Caelan urged, taking her hand and pulling her toward the exit of the alcove. "We have to move. We'll figure this out later. We can't waste any more time."

They moved quickly through the narrow tunnels, the sound of their footsteps echoing off the stone walls. The darkness seemed to close in around them, the air growing colder the farther they went. The shadows stretched, creeping along the edges of the flickering torchlight, threatening to swallow them whole.

Lyra's heart was racing, the fear clawing at her chest, but there was something else beneath it—a gnawing sense of dread, an awareness that the walls were closing in. Not just from Ivor's forces, but from the truth of the prophecy, the reality of what lay ahead. She could feel Caelan's hand tight around hers, the warmth of his fire mingling with the cold of her water, but even their combined strength felt fragile now.

"What if he's right?" she whispered, the words slipping out before she could stop them.

Caelan's grip on her hand tightened. "Don't say that. We won't let him be right. We're stronger than this."

But even as he said it, his voice lacked the conviction it had once held. They both knew it, and the truth of it hung heavy between them.

"I don't want to lose you, Lyra," he whispered, his voice raw, vulnerable. "I can't… I can't live in a world without you."

Lyra felt her throat close up, her breath catching. She stopped walking for a moment, pulling Caelan to a halt with her, her hand still clutching his. "I don't want to lose you either," she whispered fiercely, her voice full of the depth of the emotions she had been holding back. "But I can't be the one to die, Caelan. I can't. You have to promise me."

"I won't let you die," he swore, his voice fierce, full of raw intensity. "You're my everything, Lyra. I swear it. I'll fight to the end for you."

Tears filled her eyes, but she held them back, refusing to let them fall. She wanted to believe him. She wanted to believe in their love, in the strength they had found in each other. But the prophecy still loomed over them, and no matter how much they fought, no matter how much they loved each other, the truth was still there, waiting for them. One of them had to die.

The sound of the approaching army grew louder, the heavy footsteps of Ivor's men reverberating through the tunnel. Thorne was already ahead of them, his face grim, his body tense, as he prepared to make the final push to escape.

"Keep moving," Thorne urged, his voice sharper now, urgent. "We can't afford to stop."

With one last glance at Caelan, Lyra nodded, her heart heavy in her chest. They had no choice. The world outside was waiting for them, and the prophecy was closing in around them faster than they could run.

But no matter how fast they ran, no matter how far they tried to go, Lyra knew the truth. There was no escape from the darkness that followed them.

And no matter what happened, the prophecy would find them.

And it would demand its price.

# Twelve

# The Heart's Betrayal

The night air was thick with the scent of damp earth and the oppressive silence that had settled over the abandoned fortress they had taken refuge in. Caelan's eyes flickered nervously toward the flickering flames of their campfire, the light casting jagged shadows across the stone walls that seemed to close in on them, tightening their space with every passing moment. Lyra sat near him, her face illuminated by the firelight, but her expression was unreadable, distant in a way that had unsettled him since they had arrived.

He watched her, his mind torn between the need to comfort her and the overwhelming tension that gripped him. They had been through so much, fought side by side against forces that seemed insurmountable, yet something had changed. It was like a storm had passed through their relationship, leaving a trail of doubt and fear in its wake. Caelan couldn't shake the feeling that something was wrong, something that Lyra wasn't telling him.

He knew the dangers they were facing, the growing closeness of Ivor's forces, but this—this felt different. The tightness in his chest, the unease gnawing at his gut—it wasn't just the war, or the prophecy, or even the constant danger that surrounded them. It was Lyra. It was the distance that had quietly crept between them.

"Lyra," he said, his voice low, trying to bridge the space between them. "Talk to me. What's going on? You've been quiet all evening."

She didn't answer immediately. Her gaze remained fixed on the flames, her hands clenched tightly in her lap. Her lips parted as if she was about to speak, but the words didn't come. Instead, she inhaled sharply, as if bracing herself for something. When she finally looked up at him, her eyes were dark, filled with a storm of emotions Caelan couldn't quite understand.

"Caelan," she began, her voice trembling ever so slightly. "There's something I need to tell you. Something I've learned… something that has been bothering me for days."

Caelan's pulse quickened. The tension between them grew heavier, the air thick with an unspoken truth. He couldn't place the fear in her voice, but it made his chest tighten. "What is it, Lyra? Whatever it is, we can face it together."

She hesitated, her gaze shifting away from him for a moment. "I don't know who to trust anymore," she murmured, barely audible over the crackling fire. "Not even our allies."

Caelan stiffened, his heart sinking at her words. "What are you talking about?"

Her eyes locked onto his, her expression filled with a mix of sadness and determination. "I know you don't want to believe it. I didn't want to believe it either, but it's true. There's a traitor in our midst. Someone we trusted. Someone who has been feeding information to Ivor."

The words hit Caelan like a physical blow. His hand instinctively went to the hilt of his sword, his muscles tensing. A traitor? Someone in their camp working against them? The thought was unbearable.

"Who?" he demanded, his voice low and dangerous, a flicker of fire burning beneath his calm exterior. "Tell me who it is."

Lyra bit her lip, her eyes narrowing as if struggling with the weight of the revelation. "It's Thorne."

The name struck Caelan like a dagger. He felt the ground shift beneath his feet, as if the world around him had tilted. Thorne. The man who had fought by their side, who had been their ally, their trusted companion. The man who had stood beside them in battle, who had helped them escape countless close calls. A traitor?

"No," Caelan whispered, his voice hoarse with disbelief. "That can't be right. Thorne has been with us from the beginning. He's helped us. He's—"

"I know," Lyra interrupted softly, her voice breaking. "I didn't want to believe it either. But the evidence is there. The patterns. The strange messages. I've been following his movements, watching him closely, and I found proof. Proof that he's been feeding information to Ivor's forces for weeks."

Caelan's heart pounded in his chest, the words crashing over him like a wave, pulling him under. Thorne—the man who had shared their hopes, their fears—was betraying them. Was he working with Ivor from the start? Had they been played, used by someone they had trusted?

"No," Caelan repeated, though his voice was quieter now, a tremor of uncertainty creeping in. "Thorne would never…he's one of us. He believes in the cause."

Lyra shook her head, her expression filled with an aching sorrow. "He's not who we thought he was, Caelan. I found letters. Hidden messages. Everything points back to him. He's been playing us all."

A cold chill ran through Caelan's veins as he processed her words. His mind raced, trying to make sense of the impossible. The possibility of betrayal had always been a shadow hanging over them, but to have it come from someone so close, so trusted, was a reality he couldn't face.

His grip on the sword hilt tightened. "We need to confront him," he said, his voice low, filled with anger. "Now."

But Lyra placed a hand on his arm, stopping him. "No, Caelan. We can't confront him yet. We need to be sure. We need to understand why he's doing this. There's something we're missing."

He turned to her, his eyes burning with frustration. "You want me to wait? We don't have time for this, Lyra. Ivor's forces are getting closer. If Thorne is working with them, we can't afford to—"

"I know," she said quickly, her voice rising with urgency. "I know that. But we need to be smart. We need to understand what's going on before we make a mistake. If we confront him without knowing everything, we could lose everything."

Caelan clenched his fists at his sides, the fire inside him growing stronger, hotter. "I don't know if I can trust him anymore. How can you be so calm about this? How can you just let it go?"

Lyra's expression softened, her hand resting gently on his arm. "Because I need you, Caelan. I need you to stay focused. We can't let this tear us apart. Not now. Not when we're so close."

He looked at her, seeing the pain in her eyes, the strain in her voice, and something inside him cracked. The fire that had flared inside him began to settle, but it didn't extinguish. It simmered beneath the surface, ready to erupt at a moment's notice. Lyra was right. They couldn't let this betrayal tear them apart. Not now.

"I'm not letting this go, Lyra," he said, his voice low but firm. "Not until I have answers. But we'll do it your way. We'll wait."

She nodded, her relief evident in the way her shoulders relaxed slightly. But the uncertainty between them lingered, thick and oppressive, like the fog rolling in from the distant mountains.

They sat in silence for a while, the crackling fire the only sound in the otherwise still night. Lyra felt the weight of what had been revealed—what had been taken from them—sinking deeper into her chest. The betrayal wasn't just a betrayal of trust; it was a betrayal of their very foundation. They had fought for so long to build something stronger than the forces that threatened to tear them apart, but now it felt as if the ground beneath them was crumbling.

"I never wanted this," she whispered, her voice barely audible. "I never wanted to doubt him, to think that we could be so wrong about someone."

Caelan's voice was quiet but filled with understanding. "I know. I didn't either."

They were silent again, the weight of the world pressing in on them. Outside, the wind howled, the night growing colder as the shadows stretched long, swallowing up the last remnants of light. Lyra glanced over at Caelan, his profile illuminated by the firelight, his expression distant, lost in his thoughts.

She wanted to reach out to him, to make him understand that despite everything, despite the betrayal, they had to hold on to each other.

But something held her back. There was something between them now, an invisible barrier that hadn't been there before.

They had always been in this together, but now, with the weight of Thorne's betrayal hanging over them, Lyra wasn't sure if they could make it through this. The trust they had built—so carefully, so slowly—had been shaken to its core. And Caelan… the man who had always been her rock, the fire that kept her warm—she could see the doubt in his eyes. The fear.

What if he couldn't forgive Thorne? What if the betrayal tore them apart?

The thought made her chest tighten, but she pushed it aside. She couldn't afford to think like that. Not now. Not when they were so close to the end.

She could feel it in the air—the storm that was coming, the reckoning that was inevitable. Thorne's betrayal was just the beginning. There were darker truths ahead, secrets hidden beneath layers of lies and deceit, and as the flames of their love flickered between them, Lyra realized that nothing—nothing at all—would ever be the same again.

The fire crackled, sending sparks into the night, but all Lyra could hear was the sound of their fractured hearts, beating in the silence, a constant reminder that the path they were walking now was far more dangerous than anything they had faced before.

And the storm was still coming.

The night pressed down on them, as if the shadows themselves were closing in, suffocating all light, all hope. Lyra sat in the flickering glow of the fire, but the warmth from the flames didn't seem to reach her. It was as though the very essence of the world had turned cold—betrayal had seeped into their camp, and no matter how hard she tried to ignore it, the truth was suffocating.

She looked at Caelan, his face now drawn with the weight of their situation. His fiery eyes, once full of determination and confidence, now flickered with uncertainty. For the first time since she'd met him, he looked… lost. And it terrified her. She had always been able to rely on him, to draw strength from his presence, but now? Now, she wasn't sure if they would even make it through this night, let alone the war ahead.

"I don't trust him anymore, Lyra," Caelan finally spoke, his voice hollow, as if the words themselves carried the weight of his heart breaking. "I don't know if I ever did. How could I be so blind?"

His gaze fell to the ground, and for a moment, she saw the warrior—the fighter—the man who had once been so sure of himself, now standing on the precipice of doubt. He had always carried a kind of fire within him that had burned brightly, even in the darkest of times. But now it seemed to flicker, uncertain and hesitant.

Lyra's heart twisted. This wasn't just about Thorne's betrayal anymore. This was about everything. The foundation of their bond, their trust, and their love—everything had been thrown into question. She could feel the chasm opening up between them, even as they sat side by side.

"I don't know what to believe anymore," Caelan continued, his voice quiet, filled with the pain of the betrayal. "I've trusted him with my life, with yours, with everything. And now, I don't know what's real."

The agony in his voice made her want to reach out to him, to assure him, to tell him that everything would be okay. But how could she? She didn't have the answers. She didn't know what had driven Thorne to betray them, to side with Ivor—whether it was out of fear, desperation, or something darker. All she knew was that the betrayal ran deeper than they could have ever imagined.

"It doesn't make sense," Lyra said, her voice barely above a whisper. "Why would he do this? We were supposed to be in this together, Caelan. We were supposed to fight for each other."

She turned to face him, her gaze locking with his, desperate for him to see that no matter how this ended, no matter how much pain they had to endure, they couldn't let it tear them apart. Not when they were so close to the end, not when the prophecy loomed over them, threatening to swallow everything whole.

Caelan didn't meet her eyes. Instead, he stood, pacing restlessly beside the fire, the flames casting distorted shadows across his features. His movements were jerky, as though he didn't know what to do with the anger and confusion swirling inside him.

"You've always known me to be decisive," he said, his voice tight. "To know exactly what I'm fighting for. But right now? Right now, I don't even know what I'm fighting for anymore, Lyra."

Lyra stood too, her heart aching as she watched him struggle. She stepped closer, reaching for him. But when she touched his arm, he pulled away, his gaze hardening, his body bracing for something he couldn't yet name.

"Caelan," she said, her voice thick with emotion. "Please, listen to me. We're still together in this. We still have a chance to make things right. Don't let Thorne's betrayal destroy us."

But Caelan's expression softened for just a moment, and in that split second, she saw the weight of his soul, the exhaustion, the pain of everything they had been through.

"I don't know if I can forgive him," he said, his voice hoarse. "I don't know if I can forgive myself for trusting him. For letting him get so close. For believing in him when all along… all along he was working against us."

Lyra's heart squeezed. She could see the battle raging inside him—the same battle she was fighting within herself. She understood the betrayal in a way that Caelan might not. She had spent so much of her life trusting people who had turned their backs on her, on her family. But this? This was different. This wasn't just an enemy from the outside. This was a friend, a confidante, someone they had shared their hopes and fears with. A man they had trusted implicitly.

Thorne had known the truth of the prophecy, had seen the power Lyra and Caelan held, and had chosen to play both sides. Why? What had driven him to this? And what did that mean for the future of their fight?

"I can't lose you," Caelan said suddenly, his voice thick with emotion. He reached for her, his hand gripping hers with a raw urgency, as though he feared that if he let go, she would disappear. "I can't lose you to this. To the war. To Thorne's betrayal. I won't."

Lyra held his gaze, her heart hammering. She could feel the weight of his words settling inside her, sinking deep into her soul. She couldn't lose him either. The thought of it—of living in a world without him, without the fire that had always been her anchor—was unbearable.

But the truth of the prophecy still lingered between them, just out of reach, threatening to tear them apart. She had seen it. She had felt it. One of them would have to die. That was the price of unity, of peace. The cost of saving the kingdoms, of ending the war.

"I won't let you fight this alone, Caelan," she whispered, her fingers tightening around his. "Whatever it is we have to do, we do it together. We'll find a way."

He didn't respond immediately. His eyes searched hers, and in that moment, Lyra saw the depth of the battle inside him. The fire within him—the fire that had once been so sure—was now flickering, hesitant, unsure. The weight of the prophecy was pulling at him, threatening to break everything they had built.

"Do you trust me?" she asked, her voice steady despite the fear clawing at her chest.

He exhaled, his chest rising and falling with the strain of the moment. "I do," he said, his voice quiet, almost a whisper. "But trust doesn't make this any easier."

"No," Lyra said, her voice soft but firm. "It doesn't. But we can face this together. We can find a way to fight this."

He nodded, his lips pressing together as though fighting against something in himself. Then, slowly, he pulled her closer, his hand cupping the back of her head as he leaned down to kiss her—softly at first, the kiss gentle and full of unsaid promises, but then deepening as the storm inside both of them erupted. Their kiss was a desperate plea, a promise to stand together, even when the world seemed determined to tear them apart.

When they pulled apart, both breathless, Caelan rested his

forehead against hers, his chest heaving as he struggled to regain his composure.

"I don't know what's going to happen," he whispered, his voice ragged. "But I swear, I won't let anything come between us."

Lyra's heart ached with the weight of his words, but in that moment, she knew that they couldn't run from the truth any longer. The prophecy had already set its course, and they were walking a path that was both their salvation and their doom. But they would face it together. They had to.

She took a deep breath, trying to steady herself, trying to ignore the terror rising inside her. "We need to confront Thorne. We need answers."

Caelan nodded. "We'll face him together. We'll find out the truth, even if it breaks us."

But as they prepared to face the traitor in their midst, Lyra couldn't shake the feeling that the real betrayal was not just the one Thorne had committed. It was something far deeper, something hidden within the heart of the prophecy, and it was pulling them toward an ending they were powerless to avoid.

And as the night deepened around them, Lyra realized one thing—whatever they learned from Thorne, whatever truths they uncovered, it wouldn't change the fact that their world was crumbling around them. They were racing against time, against fate, and the storm of the prophecy was growing louder with every passing moment.

The path ahead was shrouded in shadows, and Lyra and Caelan were running out of time.

# Thirteen

# The Tide's Edge

The sky above was a churning mass of black clouds, thunder rolling ominously through the air, a prelude to the storm that was already tearing through the land. The battlefield stretched before them, a twisted sea of fire and water, with the two kingdoms clashing in a violent, chaotic rage. Caelan stood at the edge of the cliff, the wind biting at his face, but it wasn't the cold that made him shiver—it was the magnitude of what lay ahead.

He could see the war, the destruction unfolding before him, as Emberfall's fiery soldiers clashed with the Tidewell forces, their elemental powers colliding in devastating explosions. The roar of battle filled the air, but it was drowned by the thunder, the earth itself seeming to tremble beneath their feet.

Beside him, Lyra's presence was a constant, though her energy was distant. He could feel the tension in her, the weight of what she was about to do, of what she had been forced to do. They had spent years running from the prophecy, from the inevitable sacrifice that had been written for them. But now, the prophecy had caught up to them. The world they had fought to protect was on the brink of destruction, and their love—everything they had built together—was about to be tested in the most impossible of ways.

"We can't hold them off much longer," Caelan muttered, his voice thick with the weight of the realization. His gaze flicked from the distant battle to Lyra, her face set in determination. "Ivor's forces are pushing forward, and the artifact—it's just ahead. If he gets his hands on it, everything we've fought for, everything we've suffered for, will be destroyed."

Lyra didn't answer immediately, her eyes locked on the battlefield. She was calm, her expression unreadable, but Caelan could feel the turbulence beneath the surface. The weight of what she had to do next was hanging over her like a shadow, a dark cloud she couldn't escape.

"I'll make sure he doesn't get it," Lyra said, her voice steady but filled with an underlying tension. She stepped forward, her boots crunching against the rocky ground, the wind whipping her hair behind her. "I have to stop him, Caelan. I have to."

Caelan reached out, grabbing her arm before she could take another step. "Lyra, wait. What are you saying? You can't go alone. The artifact is guarded by more than just Ivor's forces. There's magic there—ancient, deadly magic that we don't understand. You can't face it by yourself."

But Lyra shook her head, her eyes filled with a fierce resolve. "I don't have a choice, Caelan. This is the only way."

His heart twisted in his chest as he realized the truth. She had always been the one to make the sacrifices. She had always been the one to carry the burden, even when it should have been shared between them. And now, as the war raged around them, as the prophecy loomed over them both, she was willing to put everything on the line. For him. For them. For their world.

"You're not going to face this alone," Caelan said, his voice low but firm. "I'm with you. Every step of the way."

She met his gaze, her eyes softening for a moment before she nodded. "Then we do this together. One last time."

They turned together, heading toward the heart of the battlefield, where the ancient artifact was hidden in the ruins of an old temple—an artifact that had been lost to time, its power unknown, its potential unfathomable. Ivor had been searching for it for years, driven by a lust for power that would stop at nothing to see him in control of both kingdoms. But they would stop him. They had to.

The wind howled as they made their way through the chaos, the ground beneath them shaking with the force of the battle. Lyra could feel the tug of the water beneath her skin, the power she had always struggled to control now surging with a force she could barely contain. She could see the waves crashing in the distance, crashing against the shore, their violent motion reflecting the chaos of the war.

Caelan's fire burned beside her, his presence a constant reminder of the strength they shared. His flames flickered and danced around them, guiding them through the tumultuous battlefield. But there was something different about his fire today. Something darker, more controlled, as though the weight of the prophecy had bound him in a way that was both terrifying and necessary.

They reached the temple ruins, the ancient stone columns rising from the earth like silent sentinels. The artifact was inside, hidden deep within the walls of the crumbling structure, protected by a powerful barrier that only the strongest could break. Lyra could feel its pull, the magnetic force of its power drawing her closer, but the closer they got, the more the sense of danger grew.

"Ivor's forces will be here any moment," Caelan said, his voice strained. He glanced around, his eyes scanning the ruins for any sign of movement. "We don't have much time."

Lyra nodded, her fingers already moving through the motions of the spell she had prepared. Her powers surged within her, raw and untamed, the water rising within her like a tide that could not be held back. She had never summoned this much power before, never had to wield it in such a way. It was dangerous. Reckless. But she had no choice. The world was on the edge of destruction, and she was the only one who could stop it.

She raised her hands, the water curling and twisting around her fingers, the energy flowing through her like electricity. Her magic surged, wild and untamed, but she harnessed it, shaped it, focused it toward the barrier that protected the artifact. The water roared to life, surging up the columns and around the ruins, a torrent of energy that seemed to vibrate with power.

The barrier crackled, the stone groaning as the magical shield strained against her magic. Lyra gritted her teeth, her hands trembling as the power threatened to consume her. She could feel the strain on her body, the burning in her veins, but she couldn't stop now. She couldn't afford to fail.

Behind her, she heard Caelan's voice, low and filled with worry. "Lyra, you're pushing too hard. You're going to—"

But before he could finish, the barrier shattered with a deafening crack, the sound of stone breaking like thunder, and the way was cleared. Lyra staggered back, her body trembling from the exertion. Her magic was spent, and she felt the weight of it crashing down on her, the darkness threatening to swallow her whole.

Caelan was at her side in an instant, his hand on her arm, steadying her. "You did it," he breathed, his voice filled with awe and fear. "But you're too weak. You need to rest."

"I don't have time," Lyra gasped, struggling to stay on her feet. She could feel the drain on her energy, the exhaustion threatening to pull her under. But she couldn't stop. Not now. Not when they were so close. "We have to get inside. We have to stop Ivor."

With Caelan's help, she stumbled toward the heart of the temple, the stone walls cool against her skin. The artifact was just ahead, glowing faintly in the center of the chamber, its ancient power radiating outward. It was a crystal, unlike anything Lyra had ever seen. Its surface shimmered like liquid fire, the colors shifting between red and blue, fire and water, an impossible fusion of the two elements.

Lyra reached out, her fingers brushing the surface of the crystal. The moment she touched it, a pulse of energy shot through her, and she gasped, stumbling back as the power coursed through her body. She could feel the magic, ancient and dangerous, surging within her, filling every part of her with an overwhelming heat.

And then, the door behind them crashed open. Ivor's voice echoed through the chamber, filled with fury and madness.

"You've made a mistake," he sneered, his eyes gleaming with dark satisfaction. "This power belongs to me. You should have known that, Lyra. You should have known that you were always just a pawn in this game."

Lyra turned, her vision blurring as the power of the artifact pulsed through her veins. Caelan stepped in front of her, his body a shield, his fire blazing with fury. "You won't have it, Ivor," he spat, his voice full of the anger that had burned within him since the beginning. "We won't let you destroy everything we've fought for."

Ivor's laughter echoed through the chamber, cold and menacing. "You think you can stop me? You think you can fight destiny? This is bigger than you, Caelan. Bigger than any of us."

As Ivor advanced, his hand outstretched toward the crystal, Lyra could feel the waters inside her surge again. The power was almost too much to control. It was threatening to overwhelm her, to destroy everything she had worked for, everything they had fought for. But there was no choice now. She had to make the ultimate sacrifice to stop him.

Her hands shook as she raised them, the water swirling around her, drawing the energy from the artifact. She could feel it, pulling the magic from the crystal, forcing it to bend to her will.

Caelan's voice rang out, full of desperation. "Lyra, no! You're pushing yourself too far! You can't—"

But it was too late. The waters inside her exploded outward in a tidal wave of power, crashing toward Ivor with an unstoppable force. The moment it touched him, the ground shook, the air crackling with energy.

And then, in that final moment, Lyra felt herself give way. The darkness closed in on her, her vision blurring as the power drained from her body, and the last thing she saw was Caelan's face, his expression filled with love and horror as the world around her erupted into chaos.

And then—nothing.

Lyra's body felt weightless, as though she were floating in a vast, endless sea. The pull of the water, her connection to it, was fading. Her limbs felt numb, as if the force of her magic had stripped her of everything that made her human. She tried to move, tried to breathe, but her body wouldn't respond. Her mind, too, seemed adrift, her thoughts scattered like fragile fragments in a storm.

There was nothing but darkness. No fire. No water. No Caelan. No battle. Only the oppressive silence.

But then, from the depths of that silence, there came a whisper—a distant murmur, as though someone was calling her name. Her name. *Lyra...*

It was faint, almost imperceptible, but there was something in the tone that sent a spark of warmth through her, a flicker of something she couldn't quite grasp.

*Caelan,* she thought, her heart tightening at the mere thought of him. She didn't know if she was hearing him or imagining it. But she had to find him. She had to get back to him. She couldn't leave him alone in this. She couldn't leave *them* alone.

Her thoughts became clearer, sharper, like the slow return of breath after being submerged in water. The darkness still surrounded her, but now there was a distant light—faint, but growing stronger with each passing second. It was a light that called to her, a beacon through the murk.

Her hands, trembling with the effort, pressed against the nothingness, her mind focusing on the one thing that mattered: Caelan.

She felt the sudden, violent tug of her body being pulled back to reality, the edges of her awareness snapping back into place. Her body, heavy and weak, jerked with the force of it. And then, all at once, the blinding pain surged through her, like a thousand needles embedding themselves into her skin. The energy of the artifact, the raw power of the waters that had coursed through her, was draining from her, and with it, her very life force.

She gasped, the first breath in what felt like an eternity burning her lungs. The world around her was blurry, jagged, and too bright—flickering images of fire and water, the battlefield still raging in the distance, but they felt so far removed from her now. She was lost in a haze of exhaustion, the familiar pull of magic within her barely a whisper.

And then, through the chaos, through the blur, she saw him. Caelan.

He was kneeling beside her, his hands trembling as he cupped her face, his eyes frantic with fear and pain. His usual fire was now subdued, flickering faintly, as though it were struggling to stay alight. The flames reflected the same agony that twisted his features.

"Lyra," he breathed, his voice breaking, raw with desperation. "Lyra, please."

His touch burned her, but it wasn't the comforting heat she was used to. It was a wild, uncontrolled fire, and yet it was the only thing that tethered her to the world. She tried to speak, but her lips wouldn't move, her throat dry and tight as if she were choking on her own breath.

"I can't lose you," Caelan whispered, his voice thick with tears. "Not now. Not when we're so close. Please, fight. Fight for me. For us."

Her vision swam, her body feeling as though it was being pulled in different directions—between the pulse of the artifact and Caelan's voice, between the pull of life and the inevitable call of the prophecy. She felt herself slipping again, the weight of the world pressing against her fragile form.

With every ounce of strength she could muster, she lifted her hand to his cheek, her fingers brushing against his skin. The contact was weak, but it was enough to ground him, to make him stop, to make him *see her*.

Caelan's breath caught in his throat as her fingers curled weakly against his skin. The flicker of fire within him burned brighter, fueled by the spark of hope that ignited in his chest. He held her tighter, desperate to keep her here, to keep her safe.

"I'm not going anywhere," she whispered, her voice barely a breath, a broken sound. The words were strained, as if each one took every bit of her remaining strength to speak. "I'm still here, Caelan."

His eyes locked with hers, raw, desperate, but full of that same love. The love that had burned so brightly between them, even when the world was crumbling. "Don't leave me, Lyra. Please, don't leave me."

Tears burned in his eyes, the raw emotion too much for him to contain. She saw it—the way he trembled, the way he tried to hold it all together for her. He was falling apart, and she could feel the tremor of it in her bones.

The prophecy, the weight of the decision, was still hanging over them. But right now, it didn't matter. Nothing mattered but the love between them—the love that had started it all, the love that had defied fate, that had fought against the tides of war and darkness.

She managed a faint smile, a fragile thing, but it was enough to reassure him. "I'm not leaving you, Caelan," she said, the words gaining strength as she spoke them. "I promise."

But as she spoke, something shifted within her, a faint tremor that rippled through her body. The artifact pulsed, the crystal still humming with its ancient power, and for a moment, Lyra felt as if she were being pulled back into the depths of the prophecy. The pull of its energy, its call, threatened to overwhelm her, to swallow her whole. She could feel it, the choice she had to make, the price that would finally be paid.

"No," Caelan said urgently, his voice shaking with panic. "Lyra, don't. You don't have to do this. We'll fight it. We'll figure out another way. I won't let you sacrifice yourself. Not like this."

Her heart clenched in her chest, but she knew the truth. The price had always been there, waiting for them to face it. The prophecy had already set its course, and she couldn't outrun it. She could feel it in her bones, the reality of it pressing against her heart.

"I have to," she whispered, her voice breaking. "I have to do this, Caelan. I can't let you die."

She could see the fear in his eyes, but she could also see the understanding that slowly began to seep in. They had fought for each other, for their love, for their world. But this—this was something neither of them could avoid.

The water inside her surged again, stronger now, but it wasn't just her power—it was the force of the prophecy itself, the culmination of everything they had fought for. She had to make the ultimate sacrifice.

"I love you," Lyra whispered, her voice barely a breath, but filled with all the strength she had left. "Always."

And then, as the world seemed to tilt, as the magic swirled around her like a storm, she knew the end was near. The final price of the prophecy—the final test of their love—was here.

She closed her eyes, surrendering herself to the magic, to the pull of fate.

Caelan screamed her name, but it was lost in the chaos of the moment. The world shifted violently, and then—everything went dark.

Lyra awoke to silence. There was no fire, no water. No Caelan. No war. Just a deep, empty quiet that pressed against her ears, and the soft sound of her own breath. She opened her eyes, blinking against the darkness, and realized that she was lying on the ground, the earth beneath her cold and solid.

But the moment she tried to move, a sharp pain shot through her, her body still weak from the strain of the magic. She gasped, her breath shallow, but the overwhelming sense of warmth flooded her chest, pulling her attention.

A figure stood above her, a presence she had only ever felt in the deepest parts of her heart. Caelan.

His face was the first thing she saw, his eyes filled with disbelief, hope, and fear—all of it tangled together. He was kneeling beside her, his hands gently resting on her shoulders as he held her close.

"You're awake," he whispered, his voice thick with emotion. "You're really here."

Lyra's eyes fluttered open, her hand reaching weakly to his face. "I'm here," she whispered back, her voice cracked, fragile, but filled with the love they had shared.

Caelan pulled her into his arms, holding her as though she were the most precious thing in the world, his lips pressing against her hair as he breathed her in.

"We made it," he said, his voice soft but full of reverence. "We're alive."

And in that moment, amidst the chaos and the destruction, Lyra knew one thing: no matter what the prophecy had said, no matter what it had demanded, they had survived. Together. They had won.

# Fourteen

# The Ember's Reckoning

The flames flickered and danced in the hearth, their bright orange glow casting jagged shadows across the crumbling walls of the fortress. Caelan sat on a stone bench near the fire, his hands clenched into tight fists, staring into the heart of the flames. His mind was a chaotic storm, a swirl of doubt and frustration. The fire—his fire—had always been his greatest strength. It had shaped him, defined him. It was the source of his power, his pride, his purpose. But now, the flames felt like nothing more than a curse.

He had always used his fire to protect, to fight, to shield those he loved. But now, it burned differently. It burned too hot, too fast. It felt uncontrollable, as if it was no longer something he commanded, but something that controlled him. He could still feel the heat of it inside, raging beneath his skin, ready to burst forth at the slightest provocation. And that terrified him.

He glanced over at Lyra, who was pacing across the room, her movements fluid and graceful despite the weight of the war, despite the uncertainty that had clouded their world. Her eyes were filled with determination, her posture strong, but Caelan could see the exhaustion in her, the toll that the prophecy had taken on her. He knew that she was trying to hold everything together, for both of them, but he couldn't shake the feeling that they were teetering on the edge of something they couldn't control.

The silence between them felt oppressive, thick with the unspoken words that hung in the air like smoke. The world outside was in chaos, the war raging on, but here, in the heart of the fortress, there was only the quiet hum of their powers, the flickering of the fire, and the weight of the choices that lay ahead.

"Caelan," Lyra's voice broke the silence, low and soft but carrying an undercurrent of something stronger. "What's going on? You've been distant for hours."

He didn't answer immediately, his gaze still fixed on the fire, his mind drifting back to the battle. To the artifact. To the terrible weight of the prophecy that loomed over them. But more than anything, to the fear that had started to consume him.

"I can't control it, Lyra," he said, his voice strained, as if the words were an admission of failure. "I can feel the fire, feel it burning within me, and I... I don't know if I can keep it in check anymore."

Lyra stopped in her tracks, her eyes narrowing in concern. She walked over to him, her steps measured, as if afraid that any sudden movement would cause him to break. "Caelan, you're stronger than this. You always have been."

But Caelan shook his head, the flickering shadows of the fire stretching out like tendrils, dancing on the walls. "I'm not so sure anymore." His voice was quieter now, filled with self-doubt. "I've always used my fire for good, but it feels like it's slipping away from me. It's out of control, Lyra. And I don't want to hurt you. I don't want to hurt anyone."

She knelt down in front of him, her hands gently resting on his, her touch grounding him, pulling him back to the present. "Caelan," she said softly, her voice steady and full of love, "you are not your fire. You are more than the power you wield. You are my anchor. You are the one who's always kept me grounded, even when everything around us is falling apart."

He looked up at her, his gaze filled with the uncertainty he couldn't hide. "But what if I can't control it? What if I destroy everything we've worked for? What if—"

"No," she interrupted, her voice firm, the warmth of her touch steadying him. "You won't. You *can't.*"

He opened his mouth to argue, but she placed a finger on his lips, silencing him. "Listen to me, Caelan. We've faced everything together. We've fought side by side through impossible odds. And this? This is no different. You're not alone. *We* are not alone. And the fire that you're struggling with? It's not just yours anymore. It's *ours.* It's *ours* because it's been woven into our bond, into our love. You can't walk away from that."

Caelan's heart pounded in his chest, the weight of her words sinking deep into him. He had always known, deep down, that their union was stronger than anything he had ever felt before. The fire inside him had always burned brighter in her presence. And the water, the element that was so different from his own, had always flowed in harmony with his flames, creating something… beautiful.

But now, standing at the edge of their final battle, the stakes were higher than ever. The prophecy had promised them both destruction, but it also offered them a chance to end the war, to bring peace. They couldn't afford to falter now.

"What if it's too late?" he whispered, his voice heavy with the weight of his own fears. "What if I can't control it long enough to stop Ivor? To stop everything from falling apart?"

Lyra's eyes softened, and she cupped his face in her hands, her touch gentle but unwavering. "Caelan, the only way forward is together. I need you. *We* need you."

For a moment, the world seemed to pause. The chaos of the war, the heavy weight of the prophecy, everything else faded away until there was only the two of them. He could feel her—her warmth, her power, the unbreakable bond between them—coursing through him like a river of light. He could feel the fire within him, not as something to fear, but as something to embrace.

Lyra was right. He wasn't alone in this. They weren't alone.

He closed his eyes, letting the warmth of her presence wash over him. "I can't promise that I'll be perfect," he said, his voice thick with emotion, "but I promise I'll fight for us. For this."

For the first time in hours, he felt the fire within him steady, its intensity dimming into something more manageable. He could feel the magic of the prophecy still lingering, still demanding a sacrifice, but for the first time, he didn't feel as though he were drowning in it.

Lyra's smile was soft, but it held all the strength he needed. "That's all I need, Caelan."

They sat in silence for a long moment, the fire crackling between them, its flames licking the air like a promise. They had been through so much, and now, they were on the brink of something far greater. The artifact, Ivor's forces, the fate of the kingdoms—they were all tied together by one unbreakable truth.

They were stronger together. And no matter the odds, they would face it as one.

"Let's finish this," Lyra said, rising to her feet, her hand extended to him.

Caelan stood with her, taking her hand in his, the fire and water swirling together inside them. He had always been a man of fire, but now he understood the delicate balance they had found. The fire and water could coexist, could bring balance to each other, just as they had done with each other. Together, they were unstoppable.

They moved toward the door, their hands clasped tightly, hearts beating in unison as they stepped into the unknown. The fortress outside still rumbled with the sounds of battle, the clash of armies, the roar of elemental forces, but now, there was no fear in Caelan's chest. Only resolve.

They made their way to the heart of the battlefield, their steps steady and strong. The path ahead was dark, and Ivor's forces were closing in, but they were ready. For the first time, Caelan didn't feel the weight of his fire as a burden. It was part of him, and with Lyra by his side, it was the force that would burn through any obstacle.

The artifact, the key to the war's end, lay just ahead. But the final test, the final reckoning, would be a trial not of their strength, but of their love.

As they reached the edge of the battlefield, where Ivor's forces gathered, Caelan stopped, his gaze scanning the enemy. His mind was clear now, the fire within him roaring with purpose. He knew what they had to do. They would face Ivor. Together.

"We'll stop him, Caelan," Lyra said, her voice unwavering, as she met his gaze. "We'll end this. For the kingdoms. For us."

Caelan nodded, his heart swelling with both love and determination. They had faced everything together, and now, as they faced their final challenge, he knew one thing with certainty: no matter what happened, they would never break. Not now. Not ever.

With one last breath, they stepped forward, ready to face the ultimate test of their love—and the fate of everything they held dear.

The world around them was a storm. The wind howled, carrying the distant rumble of thunder, and the air was thick with the scent of earth and fire, the unmistakable fragrance of battle. Caelan could hear the clash of swords and the cries of warriors caught in the struggle for dominance. Yet amidst the chaos, there was a calm in his chest, a steady pulse of certainty. He felt Lyra's hand in his, warm and sure, and that was all that mattered.

Together, they approached the center of the battlefield, where the ancient artifact—the key to ending the war—was said to be hidden. The massive stone temple before them rose like a dark sentinel against the wild landscape, its ruins now the heart of the fight for the future. The very air seemed to hum with power, the ground trembling beneath their feet as the final confrontation loomed.

Lyra's hand tightened around his, and for a moment, he glanced down at her, seeing the unwavering strength in her eyes. Her magic pulsed around her, the water surging within her veins like a restless tide, while his own fire burned brighter than ever. Together, they were unstoppable. They had to be.

Caelan drew in a deep breath, the smoke from the fires of war filling his lungs, and steadied himself. The power of the artifact was ahead, but so was Ivor—more dangerous than ever. The prophecy's dark shadow stretched long over them, its weight pulling at the very core of his being, but now, it no longer felt like something to fear. It was something they could challenge, something they could rewrite with their strength, their love, and their unwavering resolve.

Lyra stopped beside him, her eyes narrowing as she took in the sight of the chaos ahead. "Ivor is close," she said, her voice low but filled with a quiet fury. "He knows we're here. We don't have much time."

Caelan nodded, his grip on the sword hilt at his side tightening. "Then we make sure he doesn't reach the artifact first."

With a sharp nod from Lyra, they moved forward together, cutting through the field of battle. The clash of fire and water, of magic and steel, filled the air as Ivor's forces converged on them. Caelan could feel the heat of the flames as they swept through the battlefield, the fire licking at his skin, but he welcomed it. The power was his to command now, no longer a curse but a weapon he wielded with the purpose of protecting those he loved.

Lyra was beside him, her presence as fierce and determined as the waters that swirled within her. She raised her hands, the waves crashing around them like a mighty tide, pushing back Ivor's forces with a sheer force of will. She didn't hesitate—she was the calm within the storm, her control over the waters as sharp and exact as the fire that burned within Caelan.

"Stay close," Caelan muttered, his voice tight with determination. He could feel the power of the enemy gathering around them, but the fire inside him burned hotter, stronger, feeding off the chaos, ready to unleash.

They fought through the onslaught, the fire and water crashing together in a symphony of destruction, their powers weaving together in perfect harmony. Every swing of Caelan's sword was backed by the crackle of fire, every step Lyra took was accompanied by the surge of water, pushing forward with an unstoppable force.

But as they reached the steps of the ruined temple, a figure emerged from the shadows.

Ivor.

He stood at the top of the stairs, his eyes glowing with a malevolent light, his hands outstretched as if to command the very earth beneath them. He was the embodiment of destruction, his form wrapped in dark magic, the very air around him seeming to distort and warp with the power he held. The artifact lay just beyond him, its ancient power pulsing with a rhythm that Caelan could feel deep within his bones.

"You're too late," Ivor sneered, his voice cutting through the chaos. "The artifact is mine. And with it, I will rule both kingdoms. Your fight has been in vain."

Caelan's heart burned with fury, but Lyra's hand tightened around his, grounding him. "We'll see about that," she said, her voice unwavering.

Without another word, Ivor raised his hands, and the ground beneath them trembled as if the very earth were shifting, molding itself to his will. The wind picked up, howling like a storm, and the ground cracked open, fiery tendrils reaching up from below. It was like fighting against the very force of nature itself, and Caelan felt the weight of Ivor's power bearing down on him.

But in that moment, he felt something else—something even stronger.

Lyra.

She was by his side, her magic flowing like an unbroken current, her presence steady, unyielding. The fire inside him, once a wild, uncontrollable force, now flickered in perfect harmony with the water that surged from her. Together, they could face this. Together, they could rewrite their fate.

"I won't let you have it, Ivor," Caelan growled, stepping forward, his hand raised in defiance. "We've come too far. We've sacrificed too much. You won't take this from us."

Ivor's laugh was cold, cruel, echoing through the ruins. "You think you have control over what's happening here? You think you can stop me?" He sneered, his hands swirling with dark energy. "This prophecy was never meant to be broken. It will be fulfilled, whether you like it or not."

But Lyra, ever the calm force amidst the storm, raised her hands. "It was *never* just about the prophecy, Ivor," she said, her voice carrying a power Caelan had never heard before, a certainty that reverberated in her every word. "It was always about us. Our bond. And that's something you can never break."

The air crackled as she raised her arms, the water surging up from the depths of the earth, crashing forward in a tidal wave of energy. The ground beneath them buckled, the ancient stones groaning with the force of her power, and Ivor's dark magic faltered for a moment, just long enough for Caelan to strike.

His fire blazed to life, roaring from within him, as the sword in his hand ignited in a burst of flames, an extension of his very soul. With a roar, he charged forward, his sword slashing through the air, cutting through Ivor's dark magic as if it were paper.

Ivor howled in fury, raising a shield of shadow to block the attack. But the force of Caelan's flames was too strong, and the fire crashed against the barrier with a force that sent shockwaves through the ground. The two forces clashed, fire against shadow, light against darkness, and Caelan felt the ground tremble beneath his feet, the power of their final battle shaking the very fabric of their world.

Behind him, Lyra called forth the water, her magic pulling at the depths of the earth, the waves surging to her command. Ivor's shield shattered under the weight of their combined powers, and for a moment, time seemed to stop. The battlefield fell silent, the winds dying down, the fire and water stilling as the three forces—their powers, their choices, their fates—hung in the balance.

And then, with a final cry of defiance, Caelan thrust his sword forward, the flames bursting forth in a wave of heat and light, and the world seemed to explode in a cacophony of sound. Ivor's scream was cut short as the flames consumed him, the darkness breaking apart under the force of their combined might.

Caelan stood there, chest heaving, his body trembling with exhaustion, but his heart was steady. He had done it. They had done it.

The artifact before them pulsed with a final, brilliant light, its power now dormant, its magic fading as the forces of destruction were driven back. The storm in the distance began to calm, the winds dying down, the skies clearing.

Lyra stepped up beside him, her hand on his arm, her eyes meeting his with a quiet strength. "We did it," she whispered, her voice hoarse but full of triumph.

Caelan's heart swelled with relief, with love, with everything they had fought for. They had faced the prophecy. They had faced the darkness. And together, they had won.

And in that moment, as the last of the storm faded away, they knew that the war was finally over. The kingdom was saved. But more importantly, they had found their way back to each other. And that, more than anything, was the greatest victory they could have ever hoped for.

The battle was won, but the future—their future—was just beginning. And as they stood together, Caelan knew that no matter what the world threw at them, they would face it together. Their love, their bond, would be the fire that carried them through whatever came next.

Forever.

# Fifteen

# The Fire's Last Stand

The sun had set behind the mountains, leaving the world cloaked in an eerie twilight that felt as if it were holding its breath. The rebel forces had gathered in the shadow of the ancient ruins, where the final battle would take place. The air was thick with anticipation, and the stillness of the evening only served to heighten the tension that crackled between Caelan and Lyra. Their hands brushed briefly as they stood side by side, each feeling the gravity of the moment, but neither willing to break the silence between them.

The vast battlefield stretched before them, the ground pocked with the remnants of old battles, scars from centuries of conflict between the kingdoms of Emberfall and Tidewell. The air smelled of charred earth and smoke, and the wind carried the distant sound of clashing swords and roars of fury—signs that the armies of Ivor's forces were already preparing to descend upon them.

Caelan's gaze was fixed on the horizon, where the first hints of fire began to flicker against the sky, the glow from the distant city marking the edge of his old life. The weight of the rebellion's charge pressed down on him, a responsibility he had never sought but had grown into. His fire, the source of his strength, now felt like a threat—something too dangerous to wield without destroying the very thing he loved most. It burned in his chest, a pulsing reminder of the choices he was about to make.

Beside him, Lyra stood, her water magic simmering beneath the surface, her calm presence a stark contrast to the storm within him. She was the anchor he had always needed, the quiet force that held him steady. But the reality of what lay ahead threatened to pull them both apart. The prophecy was nearing its final chapter, and neither of them could escape its demand for sacrifice.

Caelan turned to face her, his heart heavy. "I never wanted this. Not for us. Not for you."

Lyra met his gaze, her eyes filled with quiet strength, but there was a sadness in them too. She could see the doubt gnawing at him, the fear that his fire would consume everything they had built. The fire that had once been the embodiment of his power was now a ticking bomb, its destructive potential stronger than ever.

"Caelan," she said softly, her voice barely rising above the wind, "we don't have a choice anymore. This is the only way."

The weight of her words sank into him like a blade. "And what about you? What happens to *you* when I unleash it all?"

Lyra's eyes softened, but the resolve in them remained unshaken. "I'll hold on. I'll balance you. You're not alone in this."

He shook his head, the fear in his chest growing stronger. "You don't understand, Lyra. This isn't just about us anymore. If I let it go, if I give in to the flames inside me, everything will burn. You could be consumed too."

Lyra stepped closer, her hand gently resting on his arm. "I know the risk," she said quietly. "But you're not the only one who has to face it. We do this together, or not at all."

The words struck him with the force of a revelation, as if the tension between them, the unspoken bond they had built, had finally solidified into something unbreakable. They had faced impossible odds together before, but this—this was the final test of their love, their commitment to one another. The fire would burn, but it was their union that would determine whether it would destroy them or redeem the world.

A horn sounded in the distance, breaking the silence, and the rebel forces began to stir, readying themselves for the inevitable clash with Ivor's army. The time had come.

Caelan turned back to the horizon, his eyes narrowing as the silhouette of Ivor's army loomed in the distance, marching relentlessly toward them. The flames from their torches lit up the night, casting long shadows over the field. The tension between the two armies was palpable, the air thick with the promise of violence.

"We're outnumbered," Caelan muttered, his grip on the hilt of his sword tightening. "But we have something they don't."

Lyra turned to face him, her eyes filled with purpose. "We have each other."

He nodded, taking a deep breath, and with it, a surge of fire rushed through his veins. He could feel it now, the full force of it—raging, uncontrollable, a beast he had been keeping chained for so long. But this time, the flame was different. This time, it felt like it could either save them or destroy them all.

Lyra took his hand, her touch cool against the heat of his skin. "Let's end this."

The rebel forces began their march, a sea of warriors clad in armor, their faces set with grim determination. They were ready. But as Caelan looked at them, he couldn't shake the fear that crawled beneath his skin. The cost of this battle—the price of the prophecy—loomed over them all.

Ivor's forces met them on the field, their dark banners raised high, their armies clashing in a storm of steel and fire. The battlefield erupted into chaos, but Caelan couldn't focus on anything but the heat inside him. The fire, the flame he had long kept under control, was pulsing, threatening to burst free. The power of it was unbearable, but he knew what he had to do.

The battle raged around them, and Caelan and Lyra pushed forward, cutting through the enemy lines with a blend of fire and water. Their powers flowed together—his flames burning through the darkness, her water quenching the heat where it threatened to become too much. But the deeper they moved into the battlefield, the more the flames inside Caelan roared, the more they threatened to consume him.

"I can't hold back anymore," he said through gritted teeth, his voice barely audible over the noise of the battle.

"I'm with you," Lyra said, her voice steady despite the danger. "Let it out, Caelan. We can balance it. Together."

And with that, he let go.

The fire exploded from him like a wildfire, a brilliant, blinding wave of heat and light that surged through the battlefield, cutting a path through Ivor's forces. His flames became a living, breathing thing, raging and twisting, unstoppable. He could feel the magic inside him rip through the air, the power that had once been a part of him but had now become something wild, untamed.

Lyra moved beside him, her hands raised as she called upon the waters of the earth, summoning waves of ice and liquid fire that collided with his flames in a perfect dance of balance. Her magic tempered the fire, soothing it where it threatened to burn too brightly. They were unstoppable, the fire and water working in harmony, their bond creating something more powerful than either of them could have imagined.

But even as they fought with everything they had, even as the flames roared and the waters surged, Caelan couldn't shake the fear that gnawed at him. The prophecy—the truth of it—was still there, lurking in the shadows. The final sacrifice, the cost of peace, still hung over them like a sword waiting to fall.

He turned to Lyra, his heart pounding in his chest. "I don't know how much longer I can hold it, Lyra. The fire… it's too much. It's tearing me apart."

She reached for him, her touch cool against the scorching heat of his skin. "You're not alone, Caelan," she whispered. "I'm here. I will balance you. I will keep you grounded. We *will* survive this. Together."

Her words, her touch, were the anchor he needed. The fire inside him surged again, but now, it was different. It was no longer a beast he feared. It was part of them, part of their bond. Together, they could control it. Together, they could face Ivor.

And then, from the chaos, Ivor appeared—his dark form cutting through the smoke and fire, his eyes burning with rage. He was close. Too close.

"You think you can stop me?" Ivor shouted, his voice filled with dark triumph. "You think you can control this power? You're nothing but pawns in a game you don't even understand."

Caelan's heart burned with fury. "You're wrong, Ivor. *We* understand it. The fire and water are *ours* to command, not yours."

With a roar, Ivor raised his hands, dark magic swirling around him like a storm. The ground beneath Caelan's feet cracked open, and a burst of energy shot toward him, dark and malevolent. He barely had time to react before the energy slammed into him, knocking him backward with a force that left him gasping for breath. His flames flickered and sputtered, barely contained.

Lyra was at his side in an instant, her hands raised, her water magic flowing to counter the dark energy. But even as her power clashed with Ivor's, Caelan could see the toll it was taking on her. The strain of their combined magic was too much, and the prophecy's cost was beginning to reveal itself.

"We need to finish this, now," Caelan said, his voice urgent. He could feel the fire building inside him again, hotter, more intense. He wasn't sure how much longer he could contain it. He wasn't sure if he wanted to.

Lyra turned to him, her eyes filled with a fierce determination. "Together," she said. "We can do this. We *will* do this."

With a final surge of power, Caelan released the fire within him, unleashing it in a torrent of flame that collided with Ivor's dark magic, the two forces clashing in an explosion of light and shadow. The world around them seemed to shudder as the forces collided, a storm of magic swirling between them.

In the end, it was their love, their bond, that proved stronger than the darkness Ivor sought to wield. Together, the fire and water united, their magic crashing through the chaos, destroying Ivor's power in a burst of blinding light.

And when the light faded, Ivor was gone.

The battlefield was silent. The chaos of battle had ceased, the roar of flames and crashing waves replaced by an eerie quiet. Caelan sank to his knees, the weight of everything crashing down on him. He could feel the fire still flickering inside him, but it was no longer a threat. It was a part of him, something he could control.

Lyra was beside him, her hand on his shoulder, her magic still shimmering in the air around them. She was bruised, battered, but alive.

"We did it," she whispered, her voice filled with relief.

Caelan looked up at her, his heart swelling with love and gratitude. "We did," he said, his voice thick with emotion. "Together."

And as the first rays of dawn began to break over the horizon, casting a new light over the battlefield, they knew that the war was finally over. The prophecy had been fulfilled, but at the cost of everything they had fought for.

But they had survived. They had found a way to make it through.

Together.

As the last of the flames dissipated into the morning air, the battlefield stood silent—a solemn, still moment in time. The echoes of war had faded into the distance, and the landscape was now marred by the aftermath of battle. The rebel forces, battered and bruised, had begun to regroup, their victory hard-earned, but Caelan and Lyra's fight was not yet over. The weight of what they had just faced, the cost of the prophecy, settled in their hearts like a heavy stone.

Caelan sat on the ground, his chest rising and falling with shallow breaths, his body bruised and exhausted. His hands trembled slightly from the exertion, the heat of the battle still lingering in his veins. He had wielded his fire like a weapon, felt it burn through him, over him, but it was no longer a force he feared. It was a part of him—a part of them.

But even as the battle raged around them, there was still a hollow space within him, an emptiness that had yet to be filled. He looked up at Lyra, his heart heavy with unspoken words.

Lyra stood nearby, her hands still crackling with the residual power of her water magic, her eyes scanning the battlefield. The waters of her powers shimmered in the morning light, calming now, but he could see the strain in her posture. She was just as exhausted, just as drained, but her resolve was unbroken.

She turned to him, her gaze locking onto his, and for a moment, everything else fell away. The world, the battlefield, the war—it all seemed irrelevant. There was only the two of them. Together.

"You're still here," Caelan whispered, his voice rough, barely more than a breath, but the weight of it carried so much more.

Lyra knelt down in front of him, her hands brushing the dirt from his face, the tenderness of her touch grounding him, bringing him back to himself. Her eyes softened, and despite everything—despite the devastation, despite the prophecy— they both understood. The fire inside him, the water that surged within her, was not just about destruction. It was about balance. It was about them.

"Of course, I'm here," Lyra said, her voice steady, her presence like a lighthouse in the storm. "I always will be."

Caelan closed his eyes, leaning into her touch, letting her

magic and her love soothe the burn that still lingered inside him. "I don't know how to live in a world without you, Lyra. After everything, after the fire, after the prophecy, I'm still here, but I'm not sure I'm the man I was before."

She gently cupped his face, her touch as soft as a river's current, yet there was strength in it, a grounding force that tethered him to this moment. "You don't have to be the man you were before," she whispered. "We've changed, Caelan. We both have. But I need you to understand, you are not defined by your fire. You're defined by the choices you make, by the love you give, by the man you've become."

Her words sank into him like balm to a wound, and in that instant, he knew she was right. They had changed, and perhaps, the man he was before could not stand in the face of the future they were about to build. But the man he was now, standing beside her, together—he could live with that.

"I've been so afraid," Caelan admitted, the words escaping his lips before he even realized they were there. "Afraid that my fire would destroy everything. Afraid that I would burn you. That I would burn everything."

Lyra smiled softly, her fingers gently tracing the line of his jaw. "You never did," she said quietly. "You never burned me. The fire doesn't have to be destructive. It can warm, too. It can give light in the dark."

Her words were a reminder of the truth that he had known all along, buried beneath layers of doubt and fear. Together, they could balance each other. Together, they were unstoppable. The fire, the water, their love—it was their strength. Not a curse. A gift.

Caelan pulled her closer, wrapping his arms around her, the weight of everything finally breaking free from his chest as he held her tightly. "I don't know what the future holds," he said, his voice thick with emotion. "But I know one thing for sure. I want it to be with you."

Lyra leaned her head against his chest, listening to the steady rhythm of his heartbeat, the sound of it anchoring her to the present. "And we will face it together," she whispered. "Whatever comes next."

They stayed there, in the quiet aftermath, surrounded by the wreckage of war, but for a brief moment, it felt as though time had stopped. There was no more battle, no more prophecy, no more darkness. There was only the two of them, and the unspoken promise of the future they would create together.

But the peace didn't last long. A voice called out, and they turned to find one of the rebel commanders, his face grim, his armor battered from the battle. "Caelan! Lyra!" he called, his voice urgent. "We've won, but the city's in ruins. There's still much to be done. The war is over, but the rebuilding… it's just beginning."

The weight of his words settled heavily on Caelan's shoulders. The war had been won, but the true cost was only now becoming clear. There would be no easy victory, no simple path ahead. But Caelan had never been one to shy away from a fight. And now, he had something worth fighting for.

Lyra stood beside him, her hand still tightly grasped in his. The tension in the air was palpable, but neither of them wavered. The fire and water were at their command, their strengths intertwined.

Caelan took a deep breath, standing tall, his gaze fixed on the distant horizon. "We will rebuild," he said, his voice steady, filled with the quiet strength he hadn't known he still possessed. "We will rebuild a better world, together."

Lyra's smile was faint, but it was filled with warmth, and something deeper—something eternal. "Together."

They turned back to the battlefield, where their forces were regrouping, their comrades tending to the wounded, and the fires of war were slowly dying down. The rebels had fought hard, and the kingdom—both Emberfall and Tidewell—was finally free from Ivor's tyranny.

But the true work was just beginning.

The sun began to rise over the horizon, its pale light spilling across the landscape, bathing the ruins in the glow of a new dawn. Caelan stood beside Lyra, watching as the light broke through the darkness, and for the first time in a long time, he allowed himself to believe in the possibility of hope.

The fire and water had collided, yes. But in the end, they had found balance.

And with that balance, they would create a future stronger than anything they could have imagined—together.

"Let's go," Caelan said softly, squeezing Lyra's hand. "The future awaits."

And as they walked toward the horizon, their hearts filled with the weight of what they had overcome, they knew that whatever trials the future held, they would face them as one.

## Sixteen

# The Rising Tide

The land was still smoldering. The remnants of the battle—the fires, the charred earth, the broken ruins— lay in a desolate silence, as if the earth itself were holding its breath. The sound of distant waves crashing against the shore was the only reminder that the world outside had not stopped. That life continued beyond the rubble of Emberfall and Tidewell. But here, in the wake of the devastation, it felt as if everything had come to a standstill.

Caelan stood at the edge of the ruined battlefield, his boots sinking into the ash-laden soil, his gaze fixed on the distant horizon. The sky was a pale grey, streaked with the last remnants of the blood-red sunset, and the air still held the acrid scent of smoke. The silence around him felt suffocating, like the calm before a storm. It was a stillness that held no peace, only a reflection of the world left broken in the aftermath.

Lyra stood beside him, her figure silhouetted against the

dimming light. Her face, usually full of fire and strength, was shadowed by exhaustion. The weight of what they had done, of what they had sacrificed, hung heavily between them. Neither of them spoke at first. There were no words that could capture the enormity of what had transpired, no language that could address the wound that had been carved into their hearts.

Caelan could still feel the burn of the fire inside him, but it was different now. It was quieter, more subdued, like a dying ember that could easily flare up again with the wrong touch. The flame had been a part of him, a constant companion for as long as he could remember. And now, after all that had happened, he was not sure whether it was still a blessing or a curse. The power that had once made him feel invincible now left him uncertain, questioning his every decision.

He turned to Lyra, her face drawn, her features etched with the strain of their recent battle. The water magic that had always flowed within her was quieter now, a shadow of the raging tide that had once been her strength. They had faced Ivor together, but in doing so, they had broken something—something deep within them.

"I didn't think we'd be left like this," Caelan finally said, his voice rough, the weight of his emotions pressing down on him. "I thought… I thought we would be able to rebuild. That things would get better."

Lyra's eyes flickered toward him, but she said nothing at first. Her hands were still, resting at her sides, as if she had nothing left to give. "We've won, Caelan. But it feels like we've lost everything."

The words stung, but they were true. The war was over, Ivor had been defeated, but the cost had been steep. The prophecy had demanded more than they could have ever imagined.

Emberfall and Tidewell were free from tyranny, but the people were broken, the lands scarred by centuries of war. And Caelan and Lyra? Their love had saved the kingdoms, but it had also torn them apart in ways they could not yet understand.

Caelan felt the tension in his chest tighten. He had given everything. They both had. They had risked their lives, sacrificed their hearts, and faced down the darkness that had haunted their world. And yet, standing here, amidst the wreckage of it all, there was no celebration, no sense of victory. Just the heavy weight of what they had lost.

"I feel like a stranger in my own skin," he admitted, his voice barely above a whisper. "I don't know who I am anymore."

Lyra's gaze softened, and she stepped closer to him, her presence a quiet comfort amidst the turmoil. "You're the same man you've always been, Caelan. The fire is still a part of you, but it doesn't define you. Not anymore."

He met her eyes, the truth of her words sinking in. He had spent so long letting the fire control him, letting it shape his every action, his every decision. But now, with the prophecy fulfilled, with the war behind them, he realized that he didn't need the flames to define him. He needed to find his own way forward, one that wasn't dictated by the burning force inside him.

Lyra's fingers brushed against his hand, a silent reminder that they were in this together. But even that comfort couldn't erase the distance that had grown between them in the wake of the battle. The fire and the water, once so harmonious, now felt like opposing forces. They had been pushed to their limits, their magic a volatile combination that had brought them both to the brink of destruction. How could they rebuild when the very thing that had once bound them together now seemed to tear them apart?

"We can't keep doing this," Lyra murmured, her voice strained, her gaze distant. "We can't keep fighting against each other, Caelan. Not when it feels like we're losing ourselves."

His heart clenched at her words. She was right. They had both given everything, sacrificed so much, but in doing so, they had lost a part of themselves in the process. The fire and water, their love, had been their greatest strength, but now they were left to pick up the pieces, to figure out how to live in a world that was forever changed.

"We'll figure it out," Caelan said, his voice thick with emotion. "I don't know how, but I'll find a way. For us."

Lyra looked at him, her eyes searching his, as if trying to find something she couldn't name. "And what about the kingdoms?" she asked softly. "What about the people we've fought for?"

The question hung in the air between them, heavier than the smoke that still lingered in the air. The kingdoms were free, yes, but what did that freedom really mean? The war had left scars deeper than any battle could erase. The political fallout was just beginning, and neither Caelan nor Lyra had the answers. They had fought for peace, but peace would not come easily.

"We'll rebuild," Caelan said, though his voice lacked conviction. He wasn't sure how they could rebuild when they themselves felt so broken. "We'll find a way. We *have* to."

But Lyra shook her head. "It's not just about rebuilding the kingdoms, Caelan. It's about rebuilding ourselves. We've both lost so much of who we were in the process. I don't even know where to begin anymore."

Her words struck him harder than he expected. He knew she was right. The weight of everything they had sacrificed—

everything they had given up—had left them both changed. They were no longer the same people who had stood side by side at the beginning of this journey. They had been forged in the flames of war, tempered by their love, but now, after all the destruction, they had to face the truth. The prophecy had altered them in ways they hadn't anticipated. The fire and water had both been wielded with such intensity that they could not simply go back to what they were.

The wind shifted, carrying with it the sounds of the rebuilding forces beginning to move forward. Caelan's thoughts turned to the people of Emberfall and Tidewell. They would need leaders. They would need guidance. And Caelan and Lyra—were they ready to take on that responsibility? Were they ready to lead?

"I don't want to be the leader they need," Caelan said, his voice laced with doubt. "I'm not ready. I don't know if I ever will be."

Lyra looked at him, her expression softening. "No one is ever truly ready. We make ourselves ready by doing what's necessary. By being there for those who need us."

"But we're broken," he said, his voice thick with frustration. "How can we lead when we can barely stand on our own two feet?"

Lyra's gaze was steady, her grip on his hand unwavering. "We don't have to be perfect, Caelan. We just have to be *together*. We can't fix everything overnight. But we can rebuild, piece by piece. For ourselves. For the kingdoms. For the future we want to create."

Her words, simple as they were, carried the weight of everything they had been through. She was right. They couldn't undo the past, couldn't change the choices that had led them to this point. But they could choose how they moved forward.

They had fought for love. They had fought for peace. Now, they would have to fight for themselves, for the balance they had once found but had almost lost. They had survived the prophecy, survived the destruction, but the real test was ahead. They had to find their way back to each other, to the fire and the water, and rebuild the world they had fought for.

"Together," Caelan repeated softly, his voice filled with a quiet determination. "We'll rebuild together."

Lyra nodded, her eyes meeting his, the same spark of hope flickering between them. "Together."

The first steps of their new path had begun. It wouldn't be easy, and the road ahead would be fraught with challenges, both political and emotional. But they had survived the fire and the water. And now, together, they would face whatever came next.

The sun dipped lower in the sky, casting a pale golden light over the ruined land. The shadows that had once threatened to consume them now felt distant, the horizon ahead filled with a promise of something new, something born from the ashes of what had come before.

They weren't sure what the future held. But in that moment, Caelan and Lyra knew one thing for certain: their love, their bond, would be the force that would carry them forward. And no matter the trials ahead, they would face them together.

The night settled over the battlefield, bringing with it an oppressive silence that seemed to hang in the air like a thick fog. Caelan and Lyra stood at the edge of the ruins, their hands still clasped, the weight of the world pressing down on them.

The last embers of the fire they had unleashed burned low in the distance, casting faint, flickering shadows on the ground where the battle had raged.

The sounds of the war, the clash of steel and the cries of fallen soldiers, had faded, but the emotional toll lingered in the air, thick and tangible. The kingdoms had been saved, but the cost had been so much greater than they had ever anticipated. Peace was just a distant hope now—a hope that would take more than mere words to restore.

Caelan's eyes wandered over the ruins, his gaze sweeping across the broken landscape, the bodies of the fallen rebels and Ivor's soldiers now still in the dirt. For a moment, he felt like an observer in a world that had moved on without him, as though his place in it no longer existed. He had fought to protect this world, to shield it from the darkness that had threatened to swallow it whole, but now that the battle was over, all he felt was emptiness.

Lyra was at his side, her presence steady and calming, a quiet beacon in the midst of the storm that still raged inside him. She, too, had fought for this moment. For the future they had once dreamed of. But even her unwavering strength seemed to waver now, a shadow of doubt creeping into her eyes.

"We need to get to the council," she said softly, her voice carrying the weight of the responsibilities that were beginning to fall upon them. "They need to know we're here. The people need us. We can't just stand here forever."

Caelan nodded, but the thought of facing the remnants of their kingdoms, the politics and struggles that awaited them, made his stomach twist. He wasn't sure he was ready for any of it—not the expectations, not the promises of peace that felt too fragile to hold onto. The fire that had once driven him forward was now a burden, a reminder of everything he had lost.

Lyra's hand tightened around his, grounding him, pulling him out of his thoughts. "We're going to make it through this," she whispered, her voice filled with quiet certainty. "Together."

He looked at her, really looked at her—seeing the exhaustion in her eyes, the weight of the choices they had made, the sacrifices they had both endured. She had given so much of herself, so much of her strength. Her water, once a force of pure, calm energy, had become as turbulent as the storm within her heart. She had fought not just for the kingdoms, but for him, for them, for the future they had hoped for.

"We're not the same people we were before," Caelan said quietly, his voice breaking the silence between them. "I'm not the same. The fire... it's a part of me, but it feels different now. It doesn't just burn with strength anymore. It burns with something else. Something darker."

Lyra didn't pull away. Instead, she stepped closer, her face full of empathy and understanding. "You're not alone, Caelan," she said, her voice steady but filled with emotion. "I'm here, and I'll never leave you. The fire doesn't control you. It's part of you, yes, but it doesn't have to define you. You have the power to choose."

Caelan swallowed hard, trying to steady his breath. Her words cut through the confusion, the fear that had settled in his chest. He had spent so long fighting the fire, fearing it, trying to control it. And now that it had finally been unleashed, he wasn't sure how to live with it. Was it a blessing? Or was it a curse that would forever haunt him?

"I don't know how to be the man you need me to be," he admitted, the words slipping out before he could stop them.

"I don't know if I can be that man anymore. Not with the fire inside me."

Lyra's eyes softened, her gaze unwavering. "Caelan, you've always been the man I needed," she said, her voice full of strength. "It's not the fire that makes you who you are. It's your heart. Your choices. And right now, I see you. The real you."

Her words struck him with a force that made his chest ache. The love in her voice, the belief in him—it was more than he had ever thought he deserved. She had always believed in him, even when he hadn't believed in himself. It was that love, that unwavering trust, that had brought them this far. And in that moment, he realized something that had eluded him for so long. The fire didn't have to be a curse. It could be a beacon. It could be a force for change, if only he could learn to wield it with the same care and purpose that Lyra wielded her water magic.

He took a deep breath, his hand reaching for hers once again. "I've been so afraid of what the fire could do," he said, his voice quieter now. "But I see it now. It's not about controlling it. It's about finding balance with it. With you."

Lyra smiled, the tension that had held her in place for so long easing from her shoulders. "Exactly," she whispered. "Together."

A distant horn sounded from the battlefield, drawing both their attentions. The rebel forces were beginning to move, preparing to make their way to the council chambers. They couldn't delay any longer. The future of the kingdoms, and the future they both hoped to create, depended on it.

"Let's go," Caelan said, his voice filled with newfound resolve. "We can't stand here any longer. The world is waiting for us."

They turned, their hands still entwined, and began walking toward the council grounds, the wind shifting behind them, carrying with it the first hints of dawn. The air was still heavy with the remnants of the battle, but there was something else in the air now—a quiet promise, a whisper of hope that had once seemed impossible.

As they walked, the weight of the world seemed to lift, if only for a moment. The future was uncertain, but for the first time, Caelan felt like he had a chance to shape it. With Lyra by his side, he was no longer afraid of the fire within him. Together, they would rebuild—not just the kingdoms, but themselves.

The council grounds loomed ahead, the stone steps leading up to the grand hall, where the future of Emberfall and Tidewell would be decided. The air around them was filled with murmurs, the tension in the air palpable. The leaders of the rebel forces were gathering, their faces grim as they prepared to address the outcome of the war.

Caelan and Lyra reached the foot of the stairs, their steps in sync as they made their way up. They had fought for this moment, and now they were here. But even as they climbed the steps, there was a part of Caelan that hesitated, a whisper of doubt that lingered in his chest.

Would they be able to reconcile the cost of their choices with the future they hoped to build? Could they truly move forward from the destruction they had wrought, or would the echoes of the past haunt them forever?

The doors to the council hall swung open, and Caelan stepped inside, Lyra at his side. The room fell silent as they entered, the leaders of both kingdoms and the rebel forces turning to face them. The weight of their presence was undeniable. The fire and the water—together, they had changed everything.

Caelan could feel the eyes of everyone on him, but he didn't look away. He stood tall, his hand still resting firmly in Lyra's, and together, they faced the future. The road ahead would not be easy. There would be challenges, pain, and sacrifices. But with Lyra by his side, with the love they had shared and the strength they had found in each other, he knew they could face whatever came next.

They had survived the fire and the water, and now, they would rise from the ashes, stronger than ever before.

The rising tide was no longer something to fear. It was their future—united, unstoppable, and free.

# Seventeen

# The Ember and the Tide

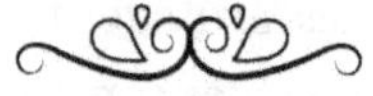

The world was broken. Not just the kingdoms of Emberfall and Tidewell, but the very earth itself. The war, the battles fought, the blood spilled—it had all led to this moment. The land lay in ruins, and in the aftermath, there was only silence. The echoes of destruction reverberated through the air, and the once-vibrant fields of Emberfall were now scorched, the waters of Tidewell tainted, their pristine clarity disrupted by the fires that had raged across the land. Even the sky above them seemed to mourn, a dull, muted grey that hung over the land like a veil of sorrow.

Caelan stood at the edge of the ravaged landscape, his boots sinking into the ash-laden soil, the fire within him burning low but steady. The flames no longer raged with reckless abandon but instead smoldered like the embers of a dying blaze, flickering weakly in his chest. He could feel the weight of the sacrifice that loomed over him, the cost of the prophecy, and the unbearable choice he would soon have to make.

Beside him, Lyra moved with the fluid grace of someone who had carried the weight of the world on her shoulders for far too long. Her eyes were shadowed, filled with the same weight he carried in his heart. The water that once flowed with ease through her veins now felt distant, its power subdued, as though the very forces of nature had turned against her. They had walked through hell together, but they knew now that the journey wasn't over. It had only just begun.

The artifact—the one thing that had been at the center of their war, their love, and their sacrifice—was waiting. Its power had always been a mystery, a secret locked in time, and now, standing on the precipice of their destiny, Caelan and Lyra were about to face its true nature. They had to go to the heart of it, deep within the ruins where it had once been hidden. It was their last chance to restore balance to a world that had been shattered.

But as the two of them prepared to move toward the artifact's resting place, a growing sense of dread filled the air around them. The path ahead was not just one of physical danger; it was a journey that would test the very core of who they were, of what they had become, and the love that had both saved and destroyed them.

Caelan's gaze shifted to Lyra, his heart heavy with the weight of the decision ahead. They had fought side by side, had defied the very forces of fate to get to this point. But the cost of what they had done—the price of the prophecy—was now more apparent than ever. The world was on the edge, and the only way to save it was to confront the artifact's true power. But that power came with a cost. The balance of fire and water, the very essence of the elements, was fractured, and only one thing could restore it.

One would have to give everything.

"We need to hurry," Lyra said, her voice steady but filled with an unspoken fear. "The longer we wait, the harder it will be to fix what's been broken."

Caelan nodded, though the words barely reached him. His mind was consumed by the thought of what lay ahead. The artifact—its power to restore balance could also destroy them. It could tear them apart, burn them to ash, drown them in the very waters they had fought to control. Every part of him screamed to turn back, to leave it all behind. But he couldn't. He couldn't abandon Lyra, couldn't walk away from the one person who had been his reason to fight, his reason to survive.

"Are you sure?" Caelan asked, his voice barely above a whisper. "Once we enter the artifact's heart, there's no going back. We might not make it out alive."

Lyra turned toward him, her eyes filled with a quiet strength that made his heart ache. "We've never gone back, Caelan. Not once. And we can't start now."

She stepped forward, her hand reaching out for him, and for a moment, everything else faded away. The war, the destruction, the choices they had made—they all felt distant, irrelevant. It was just the two of them, standing on the brink of something far greater than either of them could comprehend.

Together, they were unstoppable.

But the price of their union, the cost of the love they had forged, loomed ahead, dark and unavoidable.

"I'm ready," Caelan said, his voice filled with the quiet conviction of someone who had faced the impossible and lived. "Let's finish this."

Lyra nodded, her hand still in his, and together they moved

forward, stepping into the ruins that lay ahead. The path was treacherous, the ground uneven and cracked, remnants of the ancient temple that once held the artifact now broken and scattered. The air felt heavy with magic, as though the very earth was holding its breath, waiting for the final moment when the balance would either be restored or completely destroyed.

They reached the center of the ruins, and the artifact stood before them—a massive stone structure, its surface etched with symbols and runes Caelan couldn't comprehend. It pulsed with an otherworldly light, a deep, rhythmic thrum that seemed to reverberate through his bones. He could feel its power, raw and untamed, calling to him, pulling at his very soul.

Lyra stepped forward, her hand outstretched, her water magic already beginning to swirl around her in response to the artifact's energy. "This is it," she whispered. "This is where it all comes to an end."

Caelan's heart pounded in his chest. "Are we ready for this?"

Lyra didn't answer immediately. She only reached for his hand, pulling him toward the heart of the artifact, where the magic was strongest. The air grew thick, oppressive, and the flames inside Caelan roared to life, his body igniting with power. The artifact responded to his presence, the flames of his magic merging with the cool, steady flow of Lyra's water. Together, they were a force to be reckoned with—fire and water, chaos and calm, destruction and restoration.

As they approached the artifact, the ground beneath them trembled, the air pulsing with the magic of the ancient structure. Caelan felt the fire within him intensify, threatening to spiral out of control. He could see the waves of energy crashing around them, the force of it almost too much to bear. But Lyra's touch, cool and steady, kept him grounded. Together, they could control it. Together, they could restore the balance.

"Are you ready?" Lyra asked, her voice barely audible over the growing hum of the artifact's magic.

Caelan met her gaze, and for a moment, he saw the same fear reflected in her eyes. They both knew what had to be done. They both knew the cost. And yet, neither of them hesitated. Their love was their strength, their bond the thing that had kept them alive through every trial, every battle. They had sacrificed so much, and now, they would sacrifice everything for the greater good.

"I'm ready," Caelan whispered.

In that moment, as the power of the artifact surged around them, they knew the truth. To restore balance to the world, one of them would have to give everything. The price of peace would come at the cost of one life. The fire and water could not coexist without one of them being consumed, and the sacrifice would be inevitable. But neither of them could face the thought of losing the other.

Caelan stepped forward, his fire blazing brighter than it ever had before. The flames surged around him, threatening to overtake him, but he didn't flinch. He couldn't. Not when the world, and Lyra, depended on him.

The artifact began to glow, the light growing brighter and more intense as the power of the fire and water collided. The air around them crackled with energy, and the ground beneath them trembled, as though the earth itself were resisting the pull of their magic.

Lyra's voice broke through the roaring sound of the magic.

"Caelan, we don't have much time. The balance—it's slipping."

Caelan's heart raced.  He could feel the fire inside him burning brighter, hotter. It was too much. He could feel the magic pulling at him, threatening to consume him entirely. But he knew what had to be done. He could not let this be the end of everything they had fought for.

With a final, desperate surge of will, Caelan focused all of his fire into the heart of the artifact, sending it crashing forward, its energy meeting the flow of Lyra's water. The two elements collided with such force that the earth itself seemed to tremble beneath them. The fire and water merged in a blinding flash of light, and for a brief, heart-stopping moment, Caelan felt himself lose control, felt the fire inside him roar as though it would tear him apart.

But then, the light dimmed. The explosion of power faded, and the silence that followed was deafening.

Caelan opened his eyes, his breath coming in shallow gasps. He was still standing. He could still feel Lyra's hand in his, still feel the warmth of her touch. But something had changed. The artifact's power was still there, but it no longer pulsed with the same destructive force. The balance had been restored.

The air around them was still, quiet, the hum of magic slowly fading away.

But as Caelan looked into Lyra's eyes, he realized the terrible truth.

One of them had survived. And one of them was gone.

The world had been saved. But at what cost?

Caelan's breath hitched as he reached for Lyra, his fingers trembling, barely able to make sense of what he was seeing. She stood before him, her face pale, her eyes filled with shock, but alive. The fire had not consumed her. The water had not drowned her. Together, they had faced the artifact's devastating power—and yet, the cost was still unclear.

"Lyra?" he whispered, his voice thick with confusion and disbelief. He reached out, grasping her arm gently as though afraid she might slip away if he touched her too hard. "Lyra, are you—?"

She flinched slightly at his touch, but then her gaze steadied, and she met his eyes. Her breath was shaky, and she was clearly disoriented, but she was still standing. Alive. The artifact's light still flickered faintly behind them, but there was no sign of the catastrophic aftermath Caelan had expected.

"I—" Lyra's voice faltered, as if she were struggling to find the words. She took a breath and then spoke again, her tone shaking. "I'm… I'm still here, Caelan. But I—I don't understand."

Caelan's heart slammed against his ribs. The magic they had unleashed together had torn through him, burned through everything they had built, but still, Lyra stood beside him. The fire had threatened to take everything, yet it had left her untouched.

A wave of disbelief flooded him as his hand still rested against her, seeking her warmth, trying to ground himself in the reality that was now so fragmented. He had been ready for the sacrifice. He had steeled himself for the idea that one of them—he or Lyra—would be lost in the wake of their love. But now, standing in front of him, she was here, just as she had been before.

"I don't understand," Caelan said again, his words thick with uncertainty, his pulse racing. "We did it. We restored balance. But we—"

His voice cracked as his gaze shifted around the crumbling ruins of the artifact. It had worked. The energy around them hummed softly now, the earth beneath their feet no longer trembling with the violent pull of the two elements. The magic, the bond of fire and water, had been woven into a delicate equilibrium, but… there was something *wrong*.

"Caelan, look," Lyra interrupted, her voice urgent, her eyes wide. She stepped away from him, her feet moving cautiously toward the center of the artifact. He followed her gaze. His heart skipped a beat.

Where the artifact had once pulsed with that overwhelming, godlike power, it was now dormant—silent, and yet… something about it felt *off*. The silence that filled the air seemed too heavy, too quiet, almost unnatural.

Lyra knelt before the artifact, reaching out her hand toward the ground where the magic still lingered, almost imperceptibly. Her fingers brushed against the cool surface, and the moment she made contact, the faintest of tremors shook through the earth, reverberating up through her arm, causing her to gasp.

"Lyra?" Caelan's voice was frantic now, his hand outstretched, instinctively reaching to pull her back from the artifact. "What's happening? What is it?"

But she held up a hand, signaling him to stop. Her voice was distant, as if she were in a trance, drawn into the artifact's power once more.

"I can feel it," she whispered. "There's something else. The balance… it wasn't just restored."

Caelan's heart pounded as his mind raced. He could see her shaking slightly, her body responding to the residual power coursing from the artifact. His fire surged within him, a familiar heat rising in his chest, but now it felt like a wild beast that could not be contained. The reality of the artifact's power was dawning on him—and the consequences were far more severe than they had anticipated.

"Lyra, get away from it!" Caelan shouted, but she didn't move. The urgency in his voice seemed to slice through the chaos, but Lyra remained motionless, her hand pressed to the stone.

"It's *alive*," she murmured, her voice quivering. "It was never meant to be *fixed*—it was meant to be *contained*."

Her words hit Caelan like a blow to the chest, and before he could react, the artifact began to hum louder. The ground beneath them trembled once more, this time not with the violent fury of battle, but with the sharp, relentless pulse of something ancient, something primal. The light from the artifact flared brighter, and with a deafening crack, the stone split open.

"No…" Caelan whispered, his pulse racing. "No, no, no!"

He dove toward Lyra, pulling her away from the heart of the artifact, but it was too late. The energy surged violently, spinning like a vortex, the forces of fire and water now twisting together, melding in ways they had never been meant to.

The world around them seemed to implode. The earth cracked open beneath their feet, a violent shockwave pushing them both off balance. Caelan's fire flared wildly, instinctively trying to shield them, while Lyra's water magic erupted in a spray of light, trying desperately to hold back the chaos. But the sheer force of it was too much. The combined energies of the artifact—the fire, the water, and the ancient magic that had once been locked away—spilled forth, unstoppable.

"Caelan!" Lyra cried, her voice strained, her arms stretched out to him. "We have to stop it! It's *breaking* everything."

He could feel the flames in him rising higher, hotter, but there was nothing to control anymore. The fire and water that had once been a perfect balance now collided like opposing forces, threatening to burn them both to ash. The artifact had been an anchor, a source of power meant to restore balance, but it had been manipulated, its true nature unknown. Now, it was too unstable to control.

With one final burst of energy, the artifact shattered, and the world around them plunged into darkness.

When Caelan awoke, his body was heavy, his head pounding with the remnants of magic still lingering in the air. The ground beneath him was cold, and for a moment, he thought he was drowning. His breath was shallow, his chest constricted, and his pulse raced as panic surged within him.

"Lyra," he gasped, trying to push himself up, his body protesting. His eyes darted around, scanning the void that surrounded him. The ruins were gone. The earth was barren—dead. The artifact's presence was no longer felt. The fire inside him had been extinguished, and yet, he could still feel the remnants of its power.

"Lyra?" he called again, his voice growing more frantic as he staggered to his feet. His legs buckled beneath him, but he forced himself to keep moving. He had to find her. He had to know if she was still—

Then he saw her.

Lyra lay motionless on the ground, her face pale, her hair splayed around her like a halo. Caelan's heart dropped into his stomach, and in that instant, he thought he might collapse. He rushed to her side, his hands trembling as he knelt beside her, his fingers brushing against her cold skin.

"Lyra!" he cried, shaking her gently, but her body didn't respond. Her breathing was shallow, too shallow, and her heart rate was faint. The water that had once flowed within her was still—stilled by the artifact's uncontrolled magic.

"No, no, no," Caelan whispered, his voice breaking as he cradled her head in his lap. His hand reached for her face, his thumb brushing against her cold cheek, but there was no warmth, no life in her.

He could feel the weight of the world crashing down on him. The very thing he had fought for, the love he had tried so hard to protect, was slipping away before him. His fire was gone, his magic burned out. All that remained was a hollow emptiness, a deep sense of loss that he had never known before.

"Lyra," he whispered, tears welling in his eyes as he held her close. "Please… don't leave me."

And for a long, agonizing moment, there was nothing but the silence of the broken world around them, and the quiet sound of his heart breaking in the emptiness. The sacrifice had been made. The price had been paid. But now, Caelan was left with only the echo of their love—an echo that seemed to fade with each passing second.

Then, just when he thought he could take no more, a faint movement caught his eye. Lyra's chest rose, just the tiniest shift, and he held his breath.

Her eyes fluttered open, her lashes trembling as she took in a ragged breath. "Caelan," she murmured, her voice barely a whisper, but it was enough.

"Lyra!" he gasped, his heart soaring with relief as he pulled her close, brushing her damp hair away from her face. "You're alive."

Her eyes met his, cloudy at first, then clearing, as if her

own mind was catching up with her. She reached out weakly, her hand trembling as she touched his cheek. "I thought… I thought I was…"

Caelan's lips pressed against hers, and he pulled her closer, holding her as if she were the very thing that kept him tethered to this world. "You're here. We're both still here."

But even as he held her, he knew the truth: the cost of the balance, of the artifact, had exacted its toll. There was still so much to repair. So much left to face. And the path ahead—filled with danger, uncertainty, and sacrifice—was just beginning.

They had survived the artifact's chaos. But what came next would define them—not just as lovers, but as the very force that could rebuild a broken world.

And that world… had only just begun to heal.

# Eighteen

# The Final Sacrifice

The air was thick with anticipation. Caelan could feel it pressing against his skin, the very atmosphere alive with the energy of the final moments. His heart pounded in his chest, his breath shallow and ragged. Every step they took toward the heart of the ancient ruins seemed to echo through the cavernous silence, the weight of the world bearing down on him. The flames within him flickered weakly, a far cry from the inferno they had once been. He could feel the pull of the fire, but it was no longer the uncontrollable beast it had once been. It was subdued, a mere whisper of its former glory.

Beside him, Lyra's presence was a steady force, her cool demeanor betraying the storm raging inside her. The water that flowed within her veins seemed still, quiet, but it was only a mask. He knew her too well. She was as terrified as he was. They had faced unimaginable trials, fought battles, sacrificed so much—but now, standing at the edge of the unknown, they were confronted with the most impossible choice they had ever faced.

To restore balance to the world, to undo the devastation caused by their love and the ancient artifact, one of them would have to make the ultimate sacrifice. One of them had to give everything. And the cost of that choice—Caelan could already feel it—was going to be more than just physical. It would tear at the very fabric of who they were. It could end them. It could destroy everything they had fought for.

And yet, there was no other option.

The heart of the artifact lay ahead, its powerful presence palpable even from a distance. The stone structure seemed to pulse with an otherworldly light, casting long, shifting shadows that danced across the ground. The magic emanating from it was like a living thing, swirling and churning, an energy that could either bring them peace or obliterate them forever.

Caelan's eyes met Lyra's. Her face was illuminated by the pale glow, but the weariness in her eyes spoke volumes. They had both given so much, endured so many trials, and now the moment of truth had arrived. The world, the kingdoms, depended on them—on the balance of fire and water they had created. But at what cost?

Caelan could feel the weight of the decision crushing him. His love for Lyra, the fire that burned in his chest, and the deep bond they had shared—it was all tangled together now, impossible to untangle. How could he make this choice? How could he choose between his love for her and the world they both had fought to save?

"Caelan," Lyra's voice broke through his thoughts, soft and steady, yet tinged with sorrow. "We don't have much time."

He nodded, his throat tightening. "I know. I'm just—"

"Don't," she interrupted, her gaze sharp and unwavering. "We've been through too much to fall apart now."

Her words were a lifeline. She was right. They couldn't afford to crumble under the weight of their emotions. Not now. Not when the world was hanging by a thread.

With a final, reluctant breath, Caelan stepped forward, Lyra following closely behind. As they approached the artifact, the ground beneath them seemed to hum, the earth vibrating with power. It felt as if the very air around them was alive, the magic of the artifact reaching out, pulling them in.

"Once we do this," Caelan said, his voice hoarse, "there's no going back. This choice—it will change everything."

Lyra's gaze softened, but there was no hesitation in her eyes. She knew the stakes. She had always known. "It's not just about us anymore, Caelan. It never was. It's about the world we promised to save. It's about the future we want to give them."

He swallowed hard, his chest tightening. He didn't want to face this. Didn't want to accept the reality of what it would mean to sacrifice everything for the sake of balance. But as he looked at Lyra—her strength, her grace, the unwavering love in her eyes—he knew she was right. This was their responsibility. It was the choice they had made from the very beginning.

Together, they had defied fate. Together, they had fought for a future.

And now, together, they would make the final choice.

The artifact's energy surged, the light blinding as it pulsed with an intensity that sent a shiver through Caelan's body. The flames inside him roared to life again, but it wasn't the uncontrollable fire of before. This time, it was a different kind of fire—a controlled, focused energy that burned with purpose.

Lyra raised her hand, and water began to swirl around her, as graceful and fluid as ever. Her magic responded to the artifact's power, weaving through the air like a living thing, an extension of her very soul.

They stood before the heart of the artifact, the final barrier between them and the choice they had to make. The power within the stone was overwhelming, both fire and water mixed together, but they were stronger now. Their bond, their shared sacrifice, was enough to contain the destructive forces that swirled around them.

"This is it," Lyra said softly, her voice barely above a whisper. "We've come this far. Now, we make the final choice."

Caelan turned to her, his hand reaching out for hers, his fingers trembling as he grasped her wrist. "If we do this, Lyra... there's no coming back."

Her gaze softened, and she took a step closer to him. Her touch was gentle, but it was filled with an unshakable determination. "I know. But we've always known what the cost would be. The fire and the water were never meant to coexist without sacrifice."

He closed his eyes, the weight of her words pressing down on him. They had always known. They had always been prepared to face the consequences of their love, of the power they held together. But even now, as they stood on the edge of everything, the truth of it was almost too much to bear.

And yet, as the power of the artifact surged around them, Caelan realized something. It wasn't just the kingdoms that depended on them. It wasn't just the world they had fought for. It was them. Their love. That was the only thing that had kept them going through everything—the only thing that had made the unbearable possible. They had faced impossible odds, and together, they had survived.

This was their final test. The ultimate sacrifice. And no matter what the cost, they would face it together.

The moment stretched on, the air heavy with the decision that loomed before them.

"You've always been the fire," Lyra said, her voice steady, almost resigned. "I've always been the water. But the balance… it's never been just about us. It's about the future. About the world we leave behind."

Caelan's heart clenched in his chest, the weight of her words sinking deep into his bones. He didn't want to lose her. He didn't want to lose *them*. He had already sacrificed so much, but to lose her… It was unthinkable.

"I love you," he whispered, his voice trembling with the depth of emotion that surged through him. "I can't imagine a world without you. Without *us*."

Her fingers tightened around his, a silent promise that they would face this together. "We've never been apart, Caelan. Not truly. And we won't be now."

The ground beneath them shifted once more, the artifact's magic swirling in a final, explosive burst. The fire within Caelan flared, hot and fierce, while the waters around Lyra rose, swirling in chaotic beauty. Their powers combined, the last remnants of the fire and water entwining in a dance that only they could control.

And then, with a final, heart-stopping surge of power, the artifact's magic reached its apex, and the world seemed to hold its breath.

Caelan's heart beat faster, his body trembling with the sheer force of what was happening. He could feel the fire within him, the intense heat that threatened to consume everything. But this time, he didn't try to hold it back. He let it burn, let it flare higher than ever before. And Lyra—Lyra's magic flowed with his, a steady, calming presence amidst the chaos, holding the flames in check, allowing them to merge together.

The air around them crackled with magic, and then, at the very peak of their power, everything stilled. The energy that had been building inside them, the fire and water, finally came to a point of perfect balance. The artifact glowed brightly, its power subsiding, and the ground beneath them began to settle.

But as the light dimmed and the magic receded, Caelan and Lyra both collapsed to their knees, drained, their bodies aching with the weight of what they had just done. The fire within Caelan had burned brighter than he had ever thought possible, and the waters within Lyra had surged with more intensity than he had ever seen before.

The world around them was still, the damage they had caused now beginning to heal, but as Caelan looked at Lyra— her face pale, her body trembling—he knew that the price had been paid. The balance had been restored, but at what cost?

"Caelan," Lyra whispered, her voice hoarse. "We did it."

He nodded, his throat tight. "We did. But… at what cost?"

Lyra looked at him, her eyes filled with both sorrow and something deeper—something that reflected the love they had fought for, the bond that had never wavered, even in the face of impossible odds.

"We saved them," she said softly. "We saved *them*… and we saved each other."

Caelan looked at her, and in that moment, he realized the truth. No matter what the cost, no matter the sacrifice, they had made the ultimate choice together. And together, they had restored balance—not just to the world, but to themselves.

The fire and water had balanced. And they had, too.

The silence hung heavy between them, thick with the weight of the moment. Caelan's heart thudded painfully in his chest, but there was no denying the overwhelming sense of relief that coursed through him. The artifact, the force that had defined their journey, was no longer pulsing with that terrifying energy. It was still, its power dissipated, but the air around them still felt charged, as if the world was holding its breath, waiting for the final aftermath.

He glanced at Lyra, her face still pale, but her eyes were open, steady—filled with the same love and strength he had always admired in her. They had survived. Together.

But even as the weight of their victory settled on his shoulders, Caelan knew that the battle wasn't over. The cost of their actions—of the decision they had made together—had yet to fully reveal itself. They had restored balance, yes, but the ultimate sacrifice had already been paid. What had happened to them, to their powers? How much of what they had given up would be left in the end?

The ground beneath them was quiet, the rumbling forces that had once felt so all-encompassing now silent, as if the world itself was in a moment of awe.

"Caelan…" Lyra's voice, fragile but filled with resolve, broke the silence. Her hand reached out for his, trembling as it brushed against his wrist. "What happens now? What does this mean for us?"

Caelan closed his eyes for a moment, taking a deep, steadying breath. The fire inside him was no longer a raging inferno. It was a quiet, smoldering ember. He could still feel it, but it was a part of him now, woven into his being. The fierce heat, once so untamable, now felt like a quiet companion, as though it had settled into its rightful place.

"I don't know," he admitted, opening his eyes to meet hers. His gaze was full of uncertainty, but also something else—hope. "The artifact is gone. The world is at peace. We've done what we set out to do. But…"

He trailed off, his fingers trembling slightly as he grasped her hand more tightly. "But what does it mean for us, Lyra? Can we still be… *us?*"

Her brow furrowed in thought, her gaze distant as if searching for an answer that had not yet revealed itself. "I don't know either, Caelan. I think we've changed… more than we realize. But I also think that we've survived the hardest part."

She shifted closer, the air between them charged with an unspoken understanding. "We made a choice, Caelan. And the balance we sought was never just about the world. It was about us too."

The fire that had once consumed them both—had brought them to this moment—had been the very thing that defined their love. Their powers, fire and water, had always been opposites, yet they had always balanced each other in ways that neither of them could fully explain. Now, in this moment, after the storm had passed, Caelan realized how true that was.

"I think…" he began, his voice quiet, "that the fire and water will always be a part of us. It's who we are. But we've learned to control it together."

Lyra's gaze softened, her lips curving into a faint, wistful smile. "And maybe… we'll learn to live with the balance we've created."

Caelan nodded, a small but genuine smile tugging at the corners of his mouth. They had made it through the worst of it, and now, they would have to find their way forward. The future was uncertain, and the weight of everything they had sacrificed would stay with them. But in this moment, with Lyra by his side, Caelan found the courage to believe in their love again—the love that had defied fate, that had overcome the odds.

Just as he was about to speak again, a sudden shift in the air made him pause. The ground beneath them trembled, not violently, but with an ominous hum. Caelan turned to Lyra, his pulse quickening. Had they done enough? Had they truly restored the balance?

The artifact, now a shadow of its former self, had left its mark on the land. But was it enough? Was the cost truly paid? Or was there something else waiting for them?

Lyra's expression shifted from one of calm to alertness. She stepped back slightly, her eyes scanning the horizon. "Caelan… something's wrong."

The hairs on the back of his neck stood up as he followed her gaze. The wind, which had been eerily still, now whipped around them, rising in force. The faint glow of the artifact, dim but still present, shimmered with an unnatural intensity. The ground cracked beneath their feet, and the skies above began to swirl with dark, ominous clouds, as though the very fabric of the world were beginning to unravel.

"Lyra!" Caelan's voice shot out in alarm as the earth beneath them began to fracture. The air grew thicker, charged with raw, untamed magic that was not their own. He reached for her hand, but the energy swirling around them was too strong, pushing them apart.

"Caelan!" Lyra cried out, her voice barely audible over the growing noise of the wind and the chaotic power that surrounded them.

The world seemed to be collapsing in on itself. The fire inside Caelan flared uncontrollably, and the water around Lyra swirled in violent circles. Their powers, once perfectly balanced, now seemed to be at odds again, threatening to tear them apart. The magic that had once worked in harmony was now fighting against them, as if the universe itself was rejecting their attempts to restore order.

"What is this?" Caelan shouted, trying to shield Lyra from the chaos, but the force of the magic seemed to knock him back, sending him crashing into the ground. The fire inside him exploded, his flames consuming everything in its path, but it wasn't enough to stop the encroaching darkness. Lyra's water magic surged, but it was overwhelmed by the sheer power of the force pushing against them.

Lyra's voice broke through the storm. "Caelan! It's not us. It's the artifact. It's... *alive!*"

Caelan's heart skipped a beat. *Alive?* What did she mean?

The ground split open beneath them, and in the gaping chasm, the source of the artifact's power began to emerge. A shadowy figure, formed of swirling magic and dark energy, began to rise from the depths, its eyes glowing with malevolent light. The very air seemed to crackle with its power. It was as though the artifact, after all the destruction it had caused, had found a way to return, to reassert itself with a force that Caelan and Lyra couldn't hope to control.

"No," Caelan whispered, fear creeping into his voice. "This... wasn't supposed to happen. We *did* it. We *fixed* it!"

But Lyra's face twisted in fear as the figure in the chasm grew larger, its form slowly becoming more distinct—a monstrous figure, a being of pure, unfathomable power. It was a creature of both fire and water, its body shifting between liquid and flame, a twisted amalgamation of both elements.

The creature's eyes—glowing with an unnatural, cruel light—locked onto them. And then, in a voice that seemed to reverberate from the very core of the earth, it spoke:

"You think you have restored balance? You have *only* awakened me."

A surge of dark magic exploded from the chasm, and the world seemed to bend around them, the very air twisting in an impossible way. The ground cracked wider, the magic of the artifact, now unleashed, threatening to pull everything into the abyss.

The final sacrifice wasn't just theirs to make—it was for the entire world.

Lyra's voice trembled, but it was steady. "Caelan, we have to stop it. *Now.*"

And in that moment, Caelan understood. The choice they had made, the decision they had both carried within them, had not just restored balance—it had set the stage for a far greater conflict.

They had awakened something far darker, something far more powerful than they could have ever anticipated. And now, with the fate of everything hanging by a thread, they had no choice but to face the ultimate test.

With a final, desperate cry, Caelan and Lyra drew together, their hands clasping once more as the storm of magic surged around them. The fire and water inside them flared once more, but this time, it wasn't a battle of opposing forces. It was a fight for their very lives.

The final sacrifice was no longer a choice. It was a battle for survival. And they would have to face it—not as two elements, but as one.

**Nineteen**

# The Fire's Embrace

The air was thick with the weight of silence.

Caelan could feel it—the deep, oppressive stillness that had settled in the aftermath of the battle. The winds had stilled, the earth no longer trembled beneath his feet, and the storm of magic that had consumed them had disappeared. But in its place was an emptiness, a yawning chasm where something essential had been lost.

He stood on the edge of the ruins, the once-vibrant landscape of Emberfall now reduced to desolate ash and smoldering earth. The sky above was muted, the color of a bruised sunset, as if the very heavens mourned the sacrifices they had made. And yet, in the midst of it all, Caelan could still feel the faintest flicker of heat inside him, the remnants of the fire that had once burned so brightly—now nothing more than a faint ember in his chest.

Beside him, Lyra stood, her gaze lost in the distance. Her

once-fluid water magic had subsided, but the calm waters within her seemed to ripple in the wake of the storm they had just survived. She was still the same, and yet not. They had been through too much, had sacrificed too much, and now the world lay at their feet, broken and yet still whole.

They had done it. The balance had been restored. The prophecy fulfilled.

But at what cost?

"I didn't think it would feel like this," Caelan said, his voice hoarse. The words came out jagged, filled with emotion that he didn't quite know how to process. He could still feel the remnants of the fire that had once surged within him. But it was different now. It was… quieter. Subdued. And the empty space inside him, where the inferno had burned, felt hollow.

Lyra's eyes shifted to him, but she said nothing at first. Her expression was unreadable, but the weight of their shared experience hung heavy in the air between them. She didn't need to say it. He could see it in her eyes. The cost had been too steep for either of them to bear easily. But neither of them had the luxury of grief or regret. They had chosen this path, and they would walk it, even if they had to rebuild themselves from the ashes of what was left.

"The fire…" Caelan began, then stopped himself, taking a deep breath. He didn't know how to explain what he was feeling, or rather, what he was not feeling. The fire had always been his strength, his rage, his power. But now, it was only a shadow of its former self. The flames had been tamed, controlled, and in doing so, had left him feeling like a shell of the person he used to be. "It's not gone, Lyra. It's still here… but it's different."

"I know," she replied softly. Her voice, despite the weariness, still held its usual calm assurance. "I can feel it too."

Lyra's water magic had always been fluid, responsive. But even now, as the winds whispered around them, Caelan could sense something in her. Her once-unstoppable waves had been tempered by the sacrifices they had made, and while she still radiated strength, there was a fragility to her. She had borne the weight of their decisions as much as he had, and now the cost of their choices hung heavy on both of them.

"I thought… I thought the world would feel different once the prophecy was fulfilled," she said, her voice a quiet murmur. "I thought I would feel whole again."

"I thought I would be able to control it," Caelan replied, his tone bitter, as though the words themselves were foreign to him. "The fire. I thought I could make it mine again. But it's… it's broken."

The silence between them deepened, suffocating, filled with the raw honesty of everything they had been through. Their love had always been a spark between them—fiery, dangerous, beautiful—but now, it felt as if that spark had extinguished, leaving only the faintest glow.

And yet, despite the destruction, despite the emptiness that lingered, Caelan realized something. They had made it. Together. They had survived the storm, the sacrifices, and the chaos. And in doing so, they had created something new. Their love, tempered by fire and water, had been tested to its breaking point. But now, they stood at the threshold of a world that had been torn apart—and yet rebuilt.

"I don't know if we'll ever feel the same," Caelan whispered, his gaze never leaving her. "But I'm not afraid of that anymore."

Lyra turned to face him fully, her eyes searching his. There was a sadness in them, but there was also something deeper—a quiet strength. She had always been the steady force between them, the calming water that tamed the chaos. But now, in this moment, Caelan saw something new. She was broken, just as he was, but she was also healing. They had each been shaped by the fire and water they had wielded, and now they would have to find a way to live with the aftermath.

"I'm not afraid of that either," she said quietly. "Because even now, I can feel it. The fire, the water—they're still a part of us. Together."

Her hand reached for his, and as their fingers intertwined, something shifted within him. The ember that had once seemed so fragile, so distant, flickered again. It was faint, but it was enough. The fire hadn't been extinguished, not entirely. It had just been tempered, reshaped into something new.

Caelan took a deep breath, the weight in his chest lifting just slightly. "Do you think we can rebuild?" he asked, his voice laced with uncertainty. "Everything?"

Lyra's gaze softened as she looked out at the horizon, her eyes distant. The ruins stretched before them, but there was something in her expression that gave Caelan hope. She had always known how to find the beauty in the broken, how to make the impossible seem possible.

"I think we can," she said, her voice filled with quiet conviction. "But it's not going to be easy. We'll have to learn how to live with what we've done, with the choices we've made."

Her hand tightened around his, and Caelan squeezed back, the warmth of her touch grounding him, reminding him that they were still together. That despite everything they had lost, there was still something left to hold onto.

"I don't know what the future holds, Lyra," Caelan murmured. "But I'm willing to find out. With you."

Lyra smiled, her lips trembling slightly as she looked back at him. "I don't know either, Caelan. But I know we'll find our way."

The wind shifted, and the first rays of sunlight pierced through the clouds, casting a golden glow over the land. The world was still broken, still recovering from the devastation they had caused. But in this moment, with the fire and the water finally united within them, Caelan and Lyra knew they had a chance.

The world would heal. It had to. And with the balance restored, with their love still intact—albeit different than it had been—they could face whatever came next.

Caelan looked at Lyra, and in that moment, everything fell into place. The sacrifices they had made, the pain they had endured, had led them here—to this fragile, imperfect new beginning. They had been broken, shattered by the forces they had once controlled, but they had also found something more powerful: each other.

"You're still here," Caelan whispered, his voice thick with emotion.

Lyra nodded, her eyes brightening as a tear slid down her cheek. "I'm still here."

They stood together in the quiet aftermath, the land before them scarred but not destroyed. And though they both knew the path ahead would be difficult—filled with uncertainty and the weight of what they had sacrificed—they also knew that they would face it together. The fire and water that had once threatened to tear them apart had now become a symbol of their strength, a bond forged in sacrifice, tempered by love.

They were ready for the future. For whatever it might bring.

And as they turned to face the dawn, Caelan's heart surged

with something he hadn't felt in a long time—hope.

The wind that had once felt like a furious storm now shifted to a gentle breeze, brushing against Caelan and Lyra with a softness that was almost reassuring. The first rays of sunlight spread across the horizon, bathing the ruins in a golden hue, casting long shadows that seemed to stretch out like the tendrils of a new beginning.

They stood side by side, the weight of their journey settling into the very marrow of their bones, yet there was something else now. The remnants of their magic—the fire and water that had once been their greatest strength and their greatest burden—were now a part of them, but not in the same way they had been before. The balance they had fought for had been restored, and yet the price they had paid was still fresh in their minds. The world around them was healing, but they had changed. The sacrifice had been steep, but it was theirs to carry.

Caelan turned to Lyra, his heart aching with the unspoken words that hovered between them. He knew she could feel it too—the finality of it all. The artifact was gone, the prophecy fulfilled, and the world was on the cusp of something new. But they were left standing at the edge of it, unsure of what they would become in this new world they had created.

"We've done it," Lyra said, her voice barely above a whisper, yet there was a certainty in it that echoed the promise they had made to each other. "The balance is restored. The world will heal."

Her eyes, though filled with a quiet strength, betrayed a flicker of exhaustion. Her water magic had always been a force of calm, of fluid grace, but now, she was left to pick up the pieces of the world, just as Caelan was. The fire and the water, once so volatile and wild, now simmered beneath the surface of their souls, a constant reminder of what they had sacrificed—and what they had won.

Caelan took a step toward her, his heart swelling with love and something else—something that felt like sorrow, but not in the way he had expected. "But will we heal too, Lyra?" he asked, his voice low, filled with vulnerability he hadn't allowed himself to feel before. "Will we ever be the same again?"

For a long moment, Lyra didn't answer, her gaze drifting over the barren landscape before them. The destruction they had caused was undeniable. Emberfall's once-proud spires now lay in ruins, and Tidewell's tranquil waters were still tainted, the scars of battle not easily erased. They had given everything, and in return, the world was forever altered. The land would heal. The people would rebuild. But what about them?

She turned back to him, and for the first time, Caelan saw the raw truth in her eyes—the doubt, the fear, the unspoken weight of everything they had lost. And yet, there was also something else. A flicker of hope, of determination, of a love that refused to die.

"No," she said softly. "We won't be the same. But maybe that's not such a terrible thing. Maybe… maybe we were never meant to stay the same."

Her words struck him like a physical blow. He had always feared change—had always believed that his fire, his rage, his power, was the very thing that made him who he was. But now, standing before Lyra, he realized the truth. They had been remade, just as the world was being remade. They had sacrificed so much, but in return, they had forged something new—something stronger than the fire and water that had once separated them. They had created a new kind of balance, a new kind of love.

"But how do we move forward?" Caelan asked, his voice thick with uncertainty. "How do we find our way in a world that's been broken, when everything we knew has been changed?"

Lyra stepped closer, her fingers lightly brushing against his, the touch so familiar, so grounding, that it pulled him back from the precipice of his own doubts. "One step at a time," she said, her voice steady. "We've always moved forward, Caelan. Together."

He looked down at their hands, intertwined, the warmth of her touch anchoring him in a way that words never could. She was right. They had always moved forward, even when the path seemed impossible, even when the world itself seemed to be against them. Their love had been their guiding light, and it would continue to be. Whatever came next, they would face it together.

Caelan raised his eyes to the horizon, watching as the sun climbed higher, casting light on the broken world before them. The land was scarred, the remnants of their battle still visible, but there was hope in that light. The world was healing. And maybe, just maybe, they could heal too.

"We'll rebuild, Lyra," Caelan said, the words heavy but filled with determination. "For us. For the world. But most of all, for the love that's brought us this far."

Lyra nodded, her expression resolute, the strength in her eyes unwavering. "For us," she repeated softly. "Together."

And so, they turned together, hand in hand, facing the future that awaited them. The path ahead would be difficult, fraught with challenges they couldn't yet see, but they were no longer afraid of the unknown. They had faced the darkest corners of their own souls, had fought through fire and water, and had emerged stronger because of it.

As they walked toward the distant horizon, the sun now fully risen, the world around them seemed to stir. The first of the new green shoots began to push through the cracked earth, small but hopeful, a symbol of the life that would return in time. And as the gentle breeze carried the scent of the earth's renewal, Caelan and Lyra knew that they were not alone in this journey. They had each other. And with that, they could face anything the world threw their way.

The fire and the water had found their balance. The prophecy had been fulfilled. And now, Caelan and Lyra could begin to rebuild not just the world, but themselves.

They had made the ultimate sacrifice—but in the process, they had created a love that would endure forever, a love that would burn and flow like the very elements that had shaped them.

And as the world around them began to heal, so too would they.

Together.

# Twenty

# Between the Ember and the Tide

The sea stretched out before them, vast and endless, a horizon where fire met water, and the lines between the two were blurred by the fading light of dusk. Caelan stood at the edge of the shore, the cool breeze tugging at his dark hair, his eyes fixed on the restless waves that crashed against the jagged rocks below. The sound of the ocean was a constant, soothing rhythm—yet beneath it, there was something else, something deeper, something that resonated within him like the echo of a long-forgotten truth.

Lyra stood beside him, her presence as quiet and steady as the tide, her eyes reflecting the colors of the sea as she gazed out at the water. The winds had tousled her hair, but she didn't seem to mind. She had always been the calm in the storm, the steady hand that had kept him grounded, even when the world around them had been crumbling.

They had come to the sea for a reason, though neither of

them had spoken the words aloud. They both knew what needed to be done, even if it was the hardest thing they had ever faced. The world they had fought for, the kingdoms they had saved, were forever changed. But in the quiet between them, Caelan felt something stronger than just the weight of their past: the undeniable pull of a future they had yet to understand, but one they would face together.

They had crossed rivers of fire and water to reach this point—had given more of themselves than they ever thought possible. The sacrifice had been great, and the road had not been easy. But they were still standing. And in the end, that was enough.

"Do you think it will ever be the same?" Caelan's voice broke the silence, hoarse with the weight of everything unsaid. The words hung between them, fragile and raw, as if he were unsure whether he wanted the answer.

Lyra didn't turn to him, her gaze fixed on the horizon. The distant glow of the setting sun cast her face in shades of gold, and for a moment, Caelan didn't know if she had heard him, or if she had chosen not to respond.

"It will never be the same," she said finally, her voice soft, but resolute. "But it doesn't have to be."

The truth of her words hit him like a blow, unexpected and final. She was right. They had already crossed the point of no return. The balance of fire and water had been restored, but it had come at a cost they would have to live with for the rest of their lives. The world had been irrevocably shaped by their choices, by their love. The land, the kingdoms, even the very elements themselves had shifted, reshaped in ways they had not imagined. But the love they shared, the bond between them, that had endured.

He turned to her then, his heart aching as he looked at

the woman who had become his everything. Lyra, with her unwavering strength and gentle grace, had been his anchor in the storm. Together, they had defied fate, had torn down the walls of their destinies, and now, they stood on the edge of a new world—one they had to create, not just for themselves, but for those who would come after them.

"I don't know how to move forward from here," Caelan admitted, his voice thick with emotion. He had never been one to show vulnerability, to admit when he didn't know what came next. But here, with Lyra beside him, it felt right to be honest. To face the uncertainty together.

Lyra turned to him, her eyes searching his face as if reading his very soul. There was a quiet sadness in her gaze, but there was also something else—something stronger than the fear that had once plagued them both. It was understanding, acceptance. They had been through so much together, had sacrificed so much, and now they stood at the edge of the unknown, knowing that the future held no promises, only the strength of their bond.

"Neither of us knows," she said softly, her hand reaching out to touch his arm, grounding him. "But we don't have to know everything right now. We've survived the hardest part, Caelan. The world is broken, yes, but it can heal. And so can we."

Her words, though simple, resonated deep within him. They had been through fire and water, through pain and sacrifice, and yet they had made it through. Together. There was no question in his mind anymore, no lingering doubt that he would face whatever came next with her by his side. They had made the ultimate sacrifice, and in return, they had each other. That was all that mattered now.

The wind picked up again, swirling around them like the

very elements they had learned to control. The sea stretched out before them, endless and wild, but there was a peace in it now, as if the waves were whispering a song of renewal, of life reborn. Caelan could feel the magic of the world around him, subtle but present, like the soft pulse of life beneath his fingertips. It was as if the fire and water had found their final balance, and in doing so, had given birth to something new—something that couldn't be undone.

Lyra took a step closer to him, her fingers brushing his as she stood beside him, gazing out at the endless horizon. The golden light of the sunset bathed her in warmth, and for a moment, Caelan thought she looked like something otherworldly—like the very essence of water, both calm and powerful, capable of both destruction and creation.

"We've come so far," she said quietly, her voice almost lost in the sound of the waves crashing against the shore. "But it's not the end, Caelan. It's just the beginning."

Her words were a balm to his soul, a reminder that even in the face of all that had been lost, there was still something to build, something to strive for. The future was uncertain, but it was theirs to create. They had the power to shape it, to mold it with the lessons they had learned, with the strength they had found in each other.

"I don't know what tomorrow holds," Caelan said, his voice thick with emotion. "But I know that whatever it is, I'll face it with you."

Lyra's gaze softened, her lips curving into a small, knowing smile. "And I'll face it with you. Always."

The world around them seemed to slow, the rushing tide of the sea falling into a peaceful rhythm, the sun dipping lower in the sky, casting the world in warm, golden light. It felt like a moment suspended in time, as if the very air itself was holding its breath, waiting for them to make the next move.

And then, just as quickly as it had come, the moment passed. The sun sank beneath the horizon, leaving only the soft glow of twilight behind. The world around them was darkening, but the light they had forged together—their love, their bond— remained. It was something that could not be extinguished, not by the fire that had burned so fiercely, nor by the water that had once threatened to drown them both. It was a love that had weathered every storm and emerged stronger for it.

Caelan glanced at Lyra one last time, his heart swelling with an emotion that he couldn't quite name. She had always been his anchor, his steady force in a world that had often felt chaotic and unforgiving. But now, as they stood together at the edge of the sea, he realized that she wasn't just his anchor—she was his everything.

He reached for her hand, his fingers curling around hers, and together, they turned back toward the path that led away from the sea. The world was still broken, still healing, but they had made their choice. They would rebuild, one step at a time, knowing that the love they shared was enough to carry them forward. Together, they would face whatever came next, side by side, no matter what the world threw at them.

As they walked away from the shore, Caelan could feel the pulse of the earth beneath his feet, the steady rhythm of life returning to the world around them. The fire and water, once so wild and uncontrollable, now coexisted in perfect harmony within them. They had paid the price, but in return, they had gained something far more precious—each other.

And no matter what the future held, they would face it together, forever between the ember and the tide.

The sun had set. The night was beginning to fall, but the light of their love—steady, unyielding—shone brighter than ever.

As they walked away from the shore, the path ahead was uncertain, shrouded in the darkening night. Yet, with each step, Caelan felt a sense of clarity he hadn't known before. The fire inside him, though quiet, still pulsed with the rhythm of his heartbeat. The water that had once threatened to pull him under, that had always been Lyra's domain, now flowed gently within him, like the soft current of a river after a storm had passed.

They walked in silence for a while, their hands intertwined, the world around them still and peaceful in contrast to the chaos they had just survived. The air had grown cooler, but neither of them seemed to mind. There was warmth in their shared presence, a quiet comfort that spoke more deeply than any words could.

The land around them was healing. The earth, scarred by their battles, was beginning to show signs of recovery. Where the fires had burned, there were small shoots of new life pushing through the soil, delicate green tendrils reaching toward the sky. The sky itself, once dark with the storms of war, was now clearing, revealing the first stars of the evening. It was as if the world, too, was catching its breath, allowing itself to be reborn.

Caelan glanced over at Lyra, who seemed to be lost in her thoughts. Her eyes were distant, but there was no sadness in her gaze, only a quiet understanding. She had always known how to look beyond the surface, to see what lay beneath, and Caelan knew she was already envisioning the future, just as he was.

"Do you ever wonder if we'll be remembered for what we've done?" Caelan asked quietly, his voice breaking the stillness.

Lyra's steps slowed, and she turned to face him, her expression soft but thoughtful. "I don't know," she replied. "Maybe. Maybe not. But I don't think it matters."

Caelan frowned, the question hanging in the air between them. "But we've done so much. The world—everything—it's different now because of us."

She smiled, a small, knowing smile, and squeezed his hand. "We did what we had to do, Caelan. The world will heal, and maybe people will remember us for the choices we made, for the love we fought for. But it doesn't matter. What matters is that we are here. And we're still standing. Together."

Her words, simple yet profound, settled into his chest like the quiet settling of dust after a storm. It wasn't about being remembered. It wasn't about leaving a legacy. It was about what they had now—what they had fought for, what they had created in the chaos of everything that had come before. Their love. Their balance. Their future.

He looked at her, really looked at her, and for the first time since all of this had begun, he understood. Everything they had gone through, every sacrifice, every moment of doubt— they had faced it together. And now, as they walked into the future, there was no uncertainty in his heart. He didn't know what the future would bring. He didn't know what the world would look like in the years to come. But he knew one thing: he would face it with Lyra by his side. And that was enough.

"I don't need to be remembered," he said softly. "As long as we're together, I don't need anything else."

Lyra's smile deepened, and she leaned into him, her shoulder brushing against his. "Then let's make the most of every step we have. Together."

The world stretched out before them, vast and wild, but now it seemed full of possibilities. The pain of their past was still there, lingering in the background like the remnants of a storm, but it no longer controlled them. They had taken the darkness, the fire, and the water, and had forged something new. Something that could endure.

And so, they continued their journey, walking side by side, each step a testament to everything they had fought for—and everything they would continue to fight for.

The night grew deeper, the stars shining brightly above them, and with every step they took, the weight of the past lifted, leaving only the promise of tomorrow.

The fire and the water were no longer their enemies. They were their allies. And between the ember and the tide, Caelan and Lyra had found their place. Together, they had restored balance—not just to the world, but to their own hearts.

And in that balance, they would endure.

As the ocean waves crashed against the shore, Caelan and Lyra walked into the night, their love a steady flame, their hearts as vast as the sea.

The world, broken and rebuilt, would never be the same. But their love—born of fire and water—would endure forever.

Between the ember and the tide.